WHEN YOU ARE IN A
STRAIT-JACKET

Rev. Dr. James D. Peters, Jr.

The "eye of God" is from NASA photo of the Helix Nebula was taken by the Hubble Space Telescope. This awe inspiring image has also been featured on magazine covers and in articles about space imagery. It has been circulating since 2003.

The author sees it as depicting the fact that, in spite or his strait-jacket situation, Job's God has His eye on him.

James Russell Lowell said":

Truth Forever on the Scaffold, Wrong forever on the Throne
And that scaffold sways the future, But behind the dim unknown
Standeth God, within the shadows, keeping watch upon His own

Printed in the United States of America.

ISBN: 978-1-4669-4906-5 (sc)
ISBN: 978-1-4669-4908-9 (hc)
ISBN: 978-1-4669-4907-2 (e)

Library of Congress Control Number: 2012913206

Trafford rev. 09/12/2012

 www.trafford.com

North America & international
toll-free: 1 888 232 4444 (USA & Canada)
phone: 250 383 6864 ♦ fax: 812 355 4082

DEDICATION

Yvette Peters Rowlett

1958-2009

Thank You, Yvette, for all that God gave each of us through you. We will always love and remember you!

"Therefore we are always confident, knowing that while we are at home in the body we are absent from the Lord. For we walk by faith, not by sight. We are confident, yes well pleased rather to be absent from the body and to be present with the Lord!"

II Corinthians 5:6-8 NKJV

CONTENTS

FOREWORD

The brilliance of Dr. James D. Peters Jr. is his commitment to the art of good preaching. Fresh from seminary, I journeyed to Colorado to pursue a PhD in religion and social change at the Iliff School of Theology. Upon recommendation of my father, I was encouraged to contact Dr. Peters, then, the pastor of the New Hope Baptist Church in Denver.

I was clear in my spirit; I wanted nothing to do with pastoring or preaching. I loved the church, but I did not recognize preaching and pastoring as a gift placed upon the doorstep of my heart. Little did I know, the preaching and pastoring ministry of Dr. James D. Peters Jr. would push me to embrace the totality of my call, not just the academic and teaching segment.

Everyone in Denver knew Dr. Peters. He was a civic leader and civil rights lion of the Rocky Mountain region. New Hope Baptist Church prospered under his leadership as a church deeply connected and committed to the civic activities of Denver, Colorado. Beyond all the accolades as a leader, Dr. Peters was a lover of preaching.

Once I joined the church and eventually became Minister of Youth and assistant to the pastor, he shared with me a gift all preachers should embrace. Dr. Peters, since his initial call to ministry at age 19, had collected over 10,000 sermons in print and audio and created a written index of Sermon titles, scriptures and subjects. It was a sort of analog Google for preachers before the company became a household name. The names of John Jasper, D.E. King, Samuel DeWitt Proctor, Gardner C. Taylor, Emmanuel Scott, Sandy Ray, Charles Spurgeon, Maria Stewart, Ella Mitchell, L.K. Williams, James Jackson and Martin Luther King, Jr., populated the shelves of his library.

I was fascinated by his library and knowledge of the craft. All preachers would do well to model Dr. Peters' commitment to the study of homiletics and love for the art of African-American preaching. In this volume of messages on Job, Dr. Peters has, once again, drawn on the rich creativity of our ancestors and practical biblical insights offered in the word of God.

The power of the themes and relevancy of the Word speak to all generations. Sermons are like children—they mature grow and develop overtime. These messages were originally preached over a decade ago, but the power of the sermons has not waned but increased as economic anxiety has "strait jacketed" the dreams of the present time and place. The story of Job speaks to all walks of life, but has a special weight when preached through the personality of an elder who has the benefit of hindsight. I encourage you to allow these sermons to linger and wash over your spirit with the power of a homiletical waterfall. We are all in need in good preaching and James D. Peters Jr. provides what our hearts deeply yearn.

The Rev. Dr. Otis B. Moss III
Chicago, Ill
August 2012

ACKNOWLEDGEMENTS

I offer special thanks to Lorene Peters, my wife, whom I love and who has been at my side during all of the special moments of these years of my personal pilgrimage and who always believed that I could accomplish anything I sought to do.

To Dr. Elder and Mrs. Brenda Granger for their strong support and continuing encouragement in all of the phases of this book. It was them who, years ago, urged me to put some of my sermons in writing. After hearing this several times, I mentioned that if I did, it would be the sermon series from the book of Job, "When You Are In a Strait-Jacket". Their reply—"that was what you were preaching when we joined New Hope." I thank them from the depths of my spirit.

To my son, Tyrone Peters. The men of the Peters family have not been guardians of the nation except for Tyrone. He did it for all of us by giving a major part of his life to the Air Force for twenty-two years and in many wars. He received awards for meritorious service, (even if it meant a threat to his health), in the service to our country. He served so we could follow our favorite dreams.

To my son, James D. Peters III gave of himself in another way. He has given his life to the raising of his son James IV who was diagnosed early in life with Autism. Jim cared for him dedicating his own life, not only to little Jim, but to all children with disabilities working with lawyers, courts and with members of the U. S. Congress, and other National leaders who are deeply involved with care for people with disabilities.

To my son, Jasper D. Peters, who was here with me through this writing effort and all of his life. He has been my personal support system, guiding me through technology and so much more. He has been the one who, late at night, I could go to for spiritual direction. He believed in me and my success in many of my life's difficult times. He is the embodiment of my own spirit. In many ways, he is me and I am him.

To Rev. Rodney J. Perry for his friendship through out these productive years and helping me make it from place to place. In this life, you have few friends who have the talent necessary for the journey. We have traveled the State and Nation together preaching, teaching and attending conventions.

To Madestella C. Holcomb and Rev. William T. Golson Jr. both of whom have published and who told me where to look for the direction which I needed.

To Blanche Johnson for the years of secretarial and sermon searching support and to Jennifer Keel for the musical access and information which I needed so many times and for so many years.

To Linda Bates Leali for her editing and for her intelligence and for her staying power to get the job done.

To all of the great officers and members of the New Hope Baptist Church, of Denver, Colorado whose prayers and support have enriched my life. This most definitely includes the present pastor and first lady, Rev. Dr. Eugene and Mrs. Nichelle Downing. I also acknowledge other churches which I served as pastor: East End Baptist in Bridgeport, Connecticut,

Third Baptist in Alexandria, Virginia and Little Zion in Burke, Virginia.

To the ministers who wrote sermons and published them so that I could benefit from them for all of my ministry.

The list begins with the person who has been my own favorite preacher for over fifty years.

To Dr. Gardner C. Taylor who has been my own favorite preacher for over fifty years, and for his many, many written sermons.

To Rev. Clovis Campbell, again for his many published sermons.

To Rev. Dr. William Whatley whose sermons inspired me to do much more research than I did prior to reading his.

To Rev. Clarence E. Macartney.

To Dr. H. Beecher Hicks for "Preaching through a storm."

To Dr. Wyatt T. Walker whose many writings have lifted me in all of the seasons of my life.

To Dr. J. Alfred Smith who also published many inspirational books, not all of which were sermons.

To special friends: The late Rev. Moses W. Beasley of Alexandria, Virginia, The late Rev. Willie Davis of Las Vegas, Nevada. Rev. Carey L. Pointer of Lanham, Maryland. Rev. Dr. Otis B. Moss Jr. of Cleveland, Ohio and Rev. Dr. Otis B. Moss III of Chicago, Illinois.

May God bless you all.

When You Are In A Strait-Jacket
Sermon 1: "Asking The Wrong Questions"
By Rev. Dr. James D. Peters, Jr.

"Then the Lord said to Satan, 'Have you considered my servant Job, that there is none like him on the earth, a blameless and upright man, one who fears God and shuns evil?' So Satan answered the Lord and said, 'Does Job fear God for nothing?'" (Job 1:8-9 NKJV)

The questions from Satan to God about Job are brutally frank. For clarity, let me read them from one of the modern language versions of the Bible. The Good News Bible, Today's English version translates this passage this way. "Satan replied, Would Job worship you if he got nothing out of it? You have always protected him and his family and everything he owns. You bless everything he does, and you have given him enough cattle to fill the whole country. But now suppose you take everything he has. He will curse you to your face!" (Job 1:9-11 GNT)

Here at the beginning of the story of Job, we find, in Satan's first encounter with God, some very interesting questions being asked. Unfortunately, they are the wrong questions. To the probing mind of the inquiring student, there is the feeling that there can be no wrong questions. But that is not so in everyday life. There can be wrong, damaging, improper questions. The one asking the question here is Satan himself. He is more than just the spirit of evil, but is the enemy of every person who claims kinship in the family of God. The wrong questions are those which impugn your integrity. Wrong questions insinuate that your motives are not pure. He is saying, Lord, you give Job everything. How do you know that his motives are right? I call this asking the wrong questions.

This sermon, as we look deeply into the options and answers when you are in a strait-jacket, delves deeply into the problems, the great dangers and how to break the habit of asking the wrong questions. I have three points.

I. Things You Ought To Know About Satan

1.   Satan is no dummy, and Satan is shrewd. He is cunning, slick, and conniving. He won't come directly at you as an ugly creature, in a red suit with a long tail. Oh no. If you are looking for an ugly devil you will be fooled. He will sneak into your presence, into your life, into your home, on your job, approaching you on your blind side. He will catch you where you are weak. He has been around a long time and he knows all of the tricks.

Satan is smart, and well trained. He can think things out. He determines which weapons to use against you, how to reach you where you are vulnerable. The story is told of Satan being asked to give up some of the weapons in his arsenal. The one which he refused to give up was discouragement. With this, he said, I can tamper with people's faith. With this, I can start trouble in church or in the halls of Congress. With this I can take people to the brink of suicide.

2.   Satan has been around. He is a much traveled personification of evil from the foundation of the world. God asked Satan "where have you been?" His answer was, moving to and fro in the earth and walking up and down in it. From that, I surmise that his answer was right. In my opinion, he

was in the Garden of Eden convincing Eve to eat the apple. I also surmise that he told Abraham not to offer Isaac as a burnt offering to God. He probably interfered with Isaac. He more than likely connived with Jacob, inducing him to deceive his father and to steal his brother's birthright. Don't you think that he got Moses to spend some time looking around to see who was looking, before he killed a man?

Here are some more examples. He helped ten of the twelve spies to bring back a false report. He made Elijah afraid and caused him to run from Jezebel. He made Elisha so arrogant that he would not come out of the house after Naaman had come many miles to see him.

You see, he has been around throughout history. When Jesus went into the wilderness to fast and pray, Satan was there to taunt him. And, I am sure that when Hitler planned the unfathomable evil which led to the Holocaust and death of more than six million Jews, Satan was there. And when the horrible institution of slavery was allowed in the United States of America, in this new Republic, conceived in liberty and dedicated to the proposition that all men are created equal, Satan had to be there.

3.   In this scripture text for this sermon, when the bargain was made which put Job in this strait-jacket, it was not Job who asked the wrong questions. Job was not a party to the whole conversation or decision which would affect his life so deeply. It was Satan who asked the wrong questions. Why then do I suggest that human beings have a propensity for asking the wrong questions. You see, Satan has people working for him. When people seem to have the same mindset of Satan, they spend time working like he works. Just like Satan is restless, people working for him get just like him. When you see people who are always roaming, never satisfied, seldom happy, you wonder how they got like that. Well, possibly they got so close

to Satan that they became like him. Satan wanted to make light of, run down, and criticize any good which Job accomplished. Satan, like those who follow after him today, believes that you can build yourself up, make yourself look good, by tearing someone else down. Don't you know people like that? Have you ever been like that? Sadly there are people who are so basically evil that they are always discontent and complaining. If you look for the worst in people, you will see only the worst in them. But, if you look for the best in people, that's what you will find.

II. Questions From Which You Cannot Defend Yourself

1. A person can be sued in court for slander if they accuse someone falsely. But, when they make it a question, it usually leaves the slandered person defenseless. A question like this, "Did you hear that she . . . . ?" Anything can follow that. Or, how about these questions? "Is it true that he served time in Texas?" "Do you know why they say he left his last job?" Do you see what I mean? Nobody can prove that you are lying on someone if you just ask questions. But, you may be asking the wrong questions.

Satan questions Job's motive for serving God. He does the same thing to many of the people who are active in the church. Why are you a preacher, Satan would ask me. Is it so you can sit in the pulpit, and have people respect you as a leader where ever you go." (Maybe they give the respect at least in front of your face.) Is it just to be seen and heard. Or, why do you teach or serve on a board? Just when you are trying to do your best in and for your community, here comes Satan, or some people under his sphere of influence, asking the wrong questions.

2. Asking the wrong questions can leave the victim without a comeback response. If you accuse someone of stealing your property, you can make a legal claim and have them arrested.

But when we question someone's motive for doing good, their reason for church or community service, what can they say? It's hard to defend against charges challenging your basic values, for nobody but God can know your spiritual motives.

Satan might have said, "Lord, you give Job everything. A big house with a lake nearby, a happy family, the finest of clothes, and food with servants to care for him. Nobody has even counted all his cattle. Maybe Job is good in your sight because he goes to Temple and worships you to thank you for all your goodness to him. But what is his real reason?" Job has to spend some serious seasons of major sorrow because of Satan asking the wrong questions.

3.   Asking the wrong questions defames and slanders a person without taking any of the risks of the punishment that goes with outright accusations. The asking of the wrong questions by people who do not care about you can cause you pain when the questions they ask are questions which you don't have a way to answer. This can be a clever form of attack which makes people question your honesty and impugn your integrity. Since it is not a charge, but a question, you can't always answer them back. Let me give an example. "Are they separated? You never see them together." A wrong question. When people's marriages are in trouble, the last thing they need is people asking the wrong question. Try to be a friend, be supportive, cry with them or pray for them. But, if you have been doing it, stop asking the wrong questions.

III.   What Can You Do When People Are Asking The Wrong Questions?

1.   Your being quiet when people are being slandered by Satan urging people to ask the wrong questions, is not the proper thing to do. It is not enough to just ignore them, for they are dangerous. Gandhi said, and Martin King repeated

Rev. Dr. James D. Peters, Jr.

this statement. "Non cooperation with evil is as much a moral obligation as is cooperation with good". That is a heavy idea, but it is true. Since good people are hurt by careless statements of others, someone has to speak up. Don't you be the one to keep quiet for if you do, you are cooperating with, aiding and abetting Satan.

2.   What can you do? If you have been doing so, then stop asking wrong questions. Refrain from slander, and take no part in gossip. As you go through life, ask healing questions, helping questions.

There are some wrong questions which I can answer. You remember the wrong question from the text, "Does Job serve God for nothing?" Well, I can answer that one for myself. If you ask me, do you serve God for nothing, my answer is yes and no. [Don't you hate to hear people answer a question, yes and no.] Do I serve God for nothing? Yes. Because the religion which depends on rewards is not true religion. Real religion says, like the song: "I trust in God wherever I may be." A man named Habakkuk gave this testimony, even when he was in a strait-jacket situation. "Though the fig tree may not blossom, Nor fruit be in the vines; Though the labor of the olive may fail, And the fields yield no food; Though the flock may be cut off from the fold, And there be no herd in the stalls—Yet I will rejoice in the Lord, I will joy in the God of my salvation." (Habakkuk 3:17-18 NKJV) So, yes, I serve God for nothing.

However, I also say in answer to the question, no. Because while it is true that the religion which depends on rewards is not real religion, it is also a fact that real religion brings great rewards. God gives rewards to those who trust Him. Hebrews 11:6 says, "But without faith it is impossible to please Him, for he who comes to God must believe that He is, and that He is a rewarder of those who diligently seek Him." God gives rewards. The first Psalm makes it plain. "Blessed is the man who walks not in the counsel of the ungodly, Nor stands in the path of sinners, Nor sits in the seat of the scornful; But his delight is in the law of the Lord, And in His law he meditates day and night". And here is the reward: "He shall be like a tree Planted by the rivers of water, That brings forth its fruit in its season, Whose leaf also shall not wither; And whatever he does shall prosper". (Psalm 1:1-3 NKJV)

I don't serve God, and I don't work to make the world a better place because I want to be saved. I do it because I am already saved. How do I know that I have been saved, and that I have been born again? Satan, don't challenge me on this one by asking the wrong question. I know I've got religion. Like these words taken from "You Can't Make Me Doubt Him", a song written by Harry Jernigan:

No! You can't make me doubt Him
Cause I know too much about Him.

I know in whom I have believed, and in spite of strait-jackets, I am persuaded that He is able to keep that which I have entrusted unto him against THAT day.

I may be in a strait-jacket. I may be between a rock and a hard place. I may not know where to turn. It may seem like God has made a bargain with Satan, with me in the middle.

But—
But—
But—

Out of my love for God—
Out of my faith in God—
Out of my hope for the future—
I will give my strait-jacket testimony—
Just like Job.

Rev. Dr. James D. Peters, Jr.

The Lord gave,
And the Lord has taken away;
Blessed be the name of the Lord.

(Job 1:21b NKJV)

WHEN YOU ARE IN A STRAIT-JACKET
Sermon 2: "Does Cursing Help?"
Rev. Dr. James D. Peters, Jr.

"Then said his wife to him, 'Do you still hold to your integrity? Curse God and die'. (Job 2:9 NKJV) After this opened Job his mouth, and cursed the day of his birth." (Job 3:1 NKJV)

We need to note that there is a period of time which elapses between Chapter 2 verse 7 when Satan afflicted Job from the top of his head to the soles of his feet and verse 8 when Job's suffering is full blown. It was now clear that this affliction was not a short term, temporary affliction, but a long term, life threatening one. Job's personal physical pain was increasing every day, and his hope of ever being well along with it.

Cursing is mentioned in both of the passages of scripture which is our text for this sermon. One, the often misunderstood statement by Job's wife and the other, the clear, constant and dramatic cursing of Job himself. What lessons are there here for us? And when we, like Job, find ourselves in a strait-jacket, how will we, or how do we, respond? Do we cry? Do we complain and do we curse? And more than that, if we do curse we must look at the question, which I pose, "Does cursing help?" I have three points.

I. Job's Wife

1.   Much time had passed by and Job was still sick and getting sicker. His wife said to him, how long will you hold on to your integrity? You sit in the rottenness of worms day and night, while I am a wanderer from place to place, and from house to house, waiting for the setting of the sun, that I may rest from my labors, and from the griefs which burden me down. Job you still maintain your integrity, you still insist on your innocence. It's too late to keep on doing that. You are almost dead. Why not just curse God and die?

It does seem strange, doesn't it? Job was terribly afflicted, and apparently dying; yet his soul was filled with trust in God. His wife is suggesting that he renounce God and die.

Many things happened to Job when his day became night. One of the most interesting and most misunderstood were these words from the lips of the person who should have been nearest to him. Words, which we have all heard. Words, which seem cold and cruel and sacrilegious. Words, which perhaps you have never heard explained as I will explain them now. Words, from the lips of the wife of Job. "Curse God and die." Some commentators use this, wrongly, as a put down to all women. (See a. below) She lived in a day when people believed that to curse God, to renounce God, meant spiritual death, and right on its heels, physical death. That, like a flower cut off from its stem of growth, to curse God meant to be cut off from life. Her respect for God must have been so great that cursing God meant sure death.

2.   I believe that history and preachers, commentaries and commentators have been too hard on Job's wife. When she asked her poor, sick, miserable husband to curse God, she asked him to commit suicide. It was euthanasia, a mercy killing. She could not stand to see him suffer any more. She

not only should have been close to him, she was close to him. She had been his permanent companion. His condition was so bad that when his three friends came to see him, which happens in Job 2:11-13 (KJV), he looked so bad that they didn't even recognize him. Have you ever been to see someone so sick, that they did not look like themselves? They were so troubled when they realized that this miserable man was their friend, Job, that the Bible says that they "lifted up their voice, and wept."

If Job's suffering caused three grown men to enter a period of public weeping and wailing, imagine what it did to his wife. We have lavished sympathy and admiration on her husband, but his partner in affliction has scarcely received a glance of pity. You seldom hear anyone talk about the losses of Job's wife. Dinah, which was her name, had also been affluent, a happy mother with a happy family. Now Dinah is plunged into misery and poverty. Dinah's riches had been lost too. Those were Dinah's children too, who were killed. It was Dinah's standard of living which was suddenly changed. Dinah's once honored husband is now sitting in ashes, in sickness and corruption. In a time when a woman's chief occupation was to be wife and mother, Dinah who had it all, now suddenly had nothing. She was probably confined to special quarters with the other widows. For when a wife became a widow, she was considered to be almost an outcast.

3.   Not only that, but remember it was her husband who was being accused of terrible sins which some believed had caused his sickness. How long can a wife hear rumors about her husband? How long can she see fingers pointed at her husband? How long can she hear bitter accusations and not wonder in her own heart, what had Job done? How would you like it if it happened to you?

We also need to take a brief look at what has been termed Job's reprimand to his wife. He hints that her words are not worthy of her. He implies that she is not one of the foolish women, but that now she is speaking like one of them. Now, that's a deep statement by Job. Sometimes the most effective reprimand is to appeal to someone's sense of self-respect. When you hear someone you know well, sounding off and making a scene, you might say quietly to them, "That's not like you" or "You are smarter than that."

So, in my opinion, Job did not really put his wife down and Job did not curse God. But after his friends came and sat with him for seven days and seven nights, speaking not a word, but seeing his pain and his condition become even more severe, something happened which they had not expected. Job opened his mouth and began to curse and curse and curse.

II. Job's Cursing

1.   Then Job opened his mouth. The phase "opened his mouth" is more than just an expression out of the Hebrew experience. It is a statement used only on solemn occasions, and implies deep thought or feelings, often long held back, and finally allowed to be spoken. In Matthew 5:2 at the beginning of the Sermon on the Mount, we are told that, "And Jesus opened his mouth and taught them saying."

Already, since the beginning of his troubles, Job had twice opened his mouth to bless God and to justify God's ways. Never before until now had he opened his mouth to curse. The Bible says of Job, "And he cursed his day" meaning the day of his birth. To curse your birthday is not a very wise act, since it can have no effect on today or anything else.

But, we must remember that extreme despair does not reason. It simply gives utterance to the thoughts and wishes as they arise. We call it a state of mind in which, whatever comes up comes out. Job knew that many of his thoughts were foolish, and confesses it later on in Chapter 6, verses 1-3.

Job had suffered unparalleled calamities. He had lost nearly everything—not only property, but children; not outside things only, but health and strength. Job had brooded over his trouble, but he did not speak in haste. For seven days he had been sitting quietly, but not unconscious of what was going on around him, the sores, the excruciating pain, the around-the-clock misery.

2.   But remember, some time had passed. After seven days of silent mourning is over, and there is no prospect of relief, Job began to curse. The cursing Job did was not common every day, street corner, barber shop cursing. The cursing he did was classic. It was poetic, it was critical of the things which had happened to him. It grew out of his pain and he was angry. Whether classic or not, his cursing was cursing. He cursed, he blasted, he condemned. He cursed the day he was born and the night he was conceived.

In this way he was giving vent to the agonies of his soul, and the awful contradictions of his mind. His words were solemn, deeply painful and a reflection of his confusion. They touch something within all of us who have felt like we were in a strait-jacket. But let us not excuse all of the things which he said in the bitterness of his suffering. He is known as a man of patience, in spite of his profound cursing.

He cursed the day that they said a boy child was conceived. This meant that he was cursing the fact that he was ever born.

"Let that day be in darkness", he cried out in verse 4. The meaning is the same as saying: Let it be blotted out of the calendar. Let not God regard it from above. Remove it from the calendar and Let the light never shine upon it. In verse 5 he cries, "Let a cloud dwell upon it." In other words, he wanted the thickest clouds known to use his birthday for their time to cover the earth.

3.   And Job goes on and on cursing his own birth, condemning his mother's knees which kept him from falling when he was a baby. He questioned the knees of his mother which held him or the beasts which fed him. He demanded that "there will be no joyful voice on that day. Let there be no choirs, no pleasant music heard; no dancing or merriment." He was hurting, crying and cursing. Severe sickness can make you say things which don't even sound like you.

Job even urged others to curse. He says in verse 8, "Let them curse it who detest the day, those evil people who hate the daylight." He cries in verse 10, blasting the womb because it did not close up its doors when he was born. Here is the reason why he curses the day and the night in which he was conceived and born; because, if he had never been brought into existence, he would never have seen trouble and known the meaning of this terrible suffering.

It seems harsh that he should have wished the destruction of his own birthday, long since passed. Biblical scholars on Job understand the passage to be Job's speaking of the umbilical cord, by which the fetus is nourished in its mother's womb. He is condemning that whole birth process, saying had this not functioned properly he would have been born dead; and thus this terrible suffering would not have happened to him.

III.   Does it Do Any Good?

1.   Does cursing help? Does it do any good? Well, let's take some lessons from Job as to when, and under what circumstances, and in what direction our cursing will go, and what kind of words we might use. Well, is it alright to curse?

Will it change anything? Will it make your life better? Will it give you a better handle on your temper? Will it help you to bear your pain? Will it make your suffering easier? Will it make you hate your circumstances less? Oh, I am not going to answer all of these questions. You will have to answer them yourself. I will give some guidelines from the cursing moments of Job, which may help some of us.

2. Job's cursing came after he has waited, thought it over, pondered and prayed. So, before you curse, think it over. Job waited a week before he said anything, before he started cursing. Job's cursing was indeed classic. One commentator, writing over a hundred years ago, said "There is nothing in ancient or modern poetry equal to the entire burst of cursing which Job did. Whether in the wildness and horror of its sometimes impractical mumbling, or the unreasonable suggestions of the things which he cursed, Job said some memorable things. There is pain and passion in his words. His imagination is tremendous. Anyone who reads this classic cursing will be impressed with its drama and with how far back Job tried to go to let his friends know how much he is hurting and how unfairly he is being treated."

3. Cursing the day of and the fact of your birth makes no sense. But when you are hurting, you often make little sense. Job has not been the only one to curse the day they were born. Jeremiah did it in Jeremiah 20:14. "Cursed be the day in which I was born; let the day not be blessed in which my mother bore me!" But, I don't have to go back that far. As a boy I heard somebody sing these words:

"If I had died before I was one,
I wouldn't have had this race to run."

Well, answer the question Reverend, some of you may be saying, does cursing help? When you are in a strait-jacket situation like Job was, it might. Some people say cursing stops them from hitting. If that is the case, I would rather know that you cursed someone than hit them. For I don't think God will send you to hell for telling somebody to go there. But, apply the Job litmus test before you curse.

Job thought things over, he waited before he cursed. Job's suffering was so severe that he thought he was dying before he cursed. Most important, he cursed bygone days and his own birthday. But in all of the cursing Job did in chapter 3, he did not curse God. Whatever you do, don't give up on God. No matter how bad things get, don't turn your back on God. However difficult your circumstances, don't you dare to shake your puny fingers in the face of our omnipotent God and curse Him! If you will trust and never doubt, He will surely bring you out.

Conclusion

You see, no person can judge the value of their own life. The life which you may feel is miserable may be serving some high divine purpose. You may be suffering so that many others will not know the same pain. Your life may be a blessing to the whole human family. This was the case with Job's life. We cannot know the use and value of our lives until we see it as a finished product. This is God's world. God has a purpose for every life. You are important to God.

So, if you think that your life had not been worth the living; if you feel that you have not made a valuable contribution yet; if you feel worthless and that your living has been in vain, let me tell you something. Your life is not over. As long as life lasts, there may be things which you can still do. No wonder the song writer wrote, as I have paraphrased it to say:

"If you can help somebody as you pass along
If you can cheer somebody with a word or song

If you can tell somebody he is traveling wrong
The your living will not be in vain."

We learn a lot of lessons in the shadows of life. The night of sorrow and affliction often teach us more than the days of success and health and good times. In a time of darkness and despair, David said, "I will fear no evil; For You are with me; Your rod and Your staff, they comfort me". (Psalm 23:4b NKJV)

Every time the sun goes down, it is a promise that it's coming up again in the morning. However, it is also a promise that it will be dark for a while. I often tell people who are passing through seasons of grief and pain, that when things are going bad in their lives, and trouble seems to be their constant companion, that a better day is coming. Just trust in the Lord and learn to wait, things will get better. And, don't you know, it works every time. The God we serve is a prayer-hearing God. And "they that wait upon the Lord, shall renew their strength". (Isaiah 40:31a KJV)

(a) The lengthy rebuke of the commentator on Job's wife and of women in general, is found on page 43 in "The Pulpit Commentary" a respected commentary, printed in the late 19th century, but still widely used, of the Book of Job. I see these words as a cruel put down of Job's wife and of women in general. The author calls this section **"Temptation in the Guise of Affection"**:

"This is the second single incidence in which, in the Old Testament, woman plays a part as a tempter. There is instruction in this pointed fact. Woman is the weaker vessel, in mind as in body. She has less firmness of intellectual texture. Her weakness as well as her strength lies in feeling. She is quick in impulses, both of good and evil. She represents passion, and man represents strength. On the whole, she is less capable of strong, profound, patient convictions, less able to take a large view of questions, to look beyond the present, and immediate aspect of things. Here is a picture of a lively temper, quick to feel resentment at pain or gratitude for good; but shallow understanding, unused meditation and reflection on the deeper of life. Her language is that of haste and passion. But this serves to bring out by contrast the calm, reflective piety, the convictions established by lifelong thought and experiences of her husband."

WHEN YOU ARE IN A STRAIT-JACKET
Sermon 3: "Would You Rather Be Dead Than Alive?"
By Rev. Dr. James D. Peters, Jr.

"There the wicked cease from troubling; And there the weary are at rest." (Job 3:17 NKJV)

Job is continuing his argument that he would be better off, not having been born, or being already dead. He has cursed the day he was born and the night he was conceived. He did not curse God, which would have been crucial. But what do we do about his wishing that he was not alive?

What Job saw as a blessing which he did not have, was his not being in the grave. By thinking this, he undervalued God's great gift of life. He proceeds to suggest that he has been deprived of a blessing by being still alive. His statement was foolish. He mentions how peaceful the repose of the grave would be in which he would be able to enjoy perfect rest. I imagine he said, "If I were dead I would be able to lie still, now all I do is toss and turn all through the night. If I were not among the living, I would be like one resting on his bed after a long day of hard work." Job actually said "If I were not alive, I would be sleeping, then I would be at rest. My sleep would be untroubled. It would be a deep slumber not a series of horrible nightmares." Job's cry was in accord with the current belief that for a good person, the sleep of death is peaceful. He saw that as better than what he had at the time.

Yes, it is true, that death is the end of life's troubles. It is a final escape from being the victim of the enemies of life. There, said Job," the wicked cease from troubling and the weary be at rest". This brings me again to the subject of the sermon. Would you rather be dead than alive?

I. Those Who Would Choose Death

1.   I cannot tell you that there are not people who read these words who would answer the question by saying that they would rather be dead. Some of the reasons they would give for wanting to die are these:

> A. Life is in many ways just a test of your capacity to suffer affliction. At best, life is so short, and human beings are so powerless that there is no way to escape from the unexpected suffering of life. In every case, life involves the terrible necessity and often painful experience of dying anyway.

> B. Another reason some would give for choosing death over life is the equality to be found in death. John James Ingalls has said that "In the democracy of the dead all men at last are equal". When first I heard that statement I felt anger. But, do you know that, in retrospect, the statement has some truth in it. There is an equivalence, and there is equality, in the grave.

Death is a great leveler. In this sense, what does death teach us? It teaches us humility. It warns us against the mistreatment of any other person. It encourages patience. Then, there is the prospect, the probability, of absolute equality in the grave. In this world where prejudice lives and runs rampant against people because of their color, their religion, their sex, their physical or mental handicap, or even because of their illnesses, in the grave everyone is equal. Where now Job is spurned by his fellow citizens, were he dead they would speak well of him. Does is often amaze you of how perfect we make people seem after they are dead? He could imagine memorials, and tributes, plaques and statues, praising him if he had or could die in honor. Death is a leveler. Death puts all of us on equal ground. No matter how fancy or ordinary the casket. No matter whether few or many attend the final rites, when we are all dead we are therefore all equal. In heaven, there would be no cry of misery and no darkness or problems can ever come. Over there you will never be broke, never be hungry, never be sick.

2.   Job was also saying that in death, in heaven, he would have some dignified companionship. "I", said Job "would have been at rest with the kings and counselors of the earth. I would be, [as I shall be when I die,] with those like me who have tried to help the poor, comfort the troubled, guide the lost and lonely." He was suggesting that in heaven, in the eternal resting place, the company is always good.

The human spirit, in times of distress, longs for a society of sympathetic friends. Sometimes the loneliness of sorrow is so great that the thought of the grave presents to the sufferer a welcome relief. One of the great promises made to the saints of God on earth is life after death as compensation for the blessings denied on earth.

In the grave the oppressors of human beings cease from irritating, and harassing, and distressing their fellow creatures. Those who were worn out with life can look forward to the day when the weary shall be at rest. The troubler and the troubled, the restless and the submissive, are both put into a condition of perfect peace.

3.   Yes, Job was right when he suggested that the grave is a great equalizer. The well-known and the unknown are the same there. All kinds of people and human conditions are equally blended in the grave. The grave is the appointed place of rendezvous, where all travelers meet. Equality is absolute among the children of men in their entrance into and exit from the world. All human beings begin and end life alike. Thinking about this should equally humble everybody. But, does this make it right for Job, or any of us to prefer being dead than alive?

II.   Nobody Wants to Die

1.   You may recall that line from an old popular song which said, "everybody wants to go to heaven, but nobody wants to die." It is better to suffer the pain we have than to wish we were dead. It is well to look carefully at all that we either think or speak in time of trouble. Even if you are in turmoil and covered with sores from head to toe, as Job was, you should not wish for or desire death. Life is a gift from God, even if you seem to have more than your share of temporary or seemingly permanent trouble.

There are some people who find joy in tormenting other people. As long as they live, nothing satisfies them. They are always in trouble themselves and always causing trouble for others. If you have people in your life, in your circle of friends, who are trying to bring you down, always putting you down, making you think less of yourself, you don't need those kinds of people in your life. But, you don't have to die to get away from them.

2.   What is at the root of the mind-set which makes the grave seem desirable? Yes, you may be in a difficult, strait-jacket situation right now, but just hold on, help is coming. Your Christian faith offers something better than just the peace of the

grave. Job is merely giving a voice to his personal suffering. He wants to get away from the pain. Christ offers more than momentary relief from the troubles of this life. He offers us eternal life. To the Christian, death is not sinking into silence forever, but sleeping in Christ is to awake in a new resurrected life. Job looked forward to the still, quiet, peaceful grave. But we can anticipate the blessed heaven.

Death is not the door to heaven, Christ is that door. The life eternal which we seek is better than rest. We can be born from above, to be able to walk the earth in the footsteps of Jesus. If this is what we are doing, it is not for us to long for death, but rather to do as Jesus said, "I must work the works of Him that sent me, while it is day, for the night comes when no man can work." (John 9:4 KJV)

3.   Job faced at this season of his life, the utter extinction of hope. It is said that "the miserable have no other medicine, but hope." Hope—that things will eventually improve; Hope—that the clouds of sickness will give way to the fair sunshine of health. But even this hope is something which Job seems to have abandoned. It would be incorrect to affirm that Job has completely lost his hold on God, but at this point he has no hope of a return to health and happiness.

Yet, in this, Job made a spiritual misstep. He erred first in thinking that he was at his worst point. True, things were bad. But, when things seem to be at their worst in your life, you need to know that it still could be worse. You have a lot to thank God for, no matter how rough things are, because they could be worse. Everything that he knew and was important to him seemed to be gone, but there was still breath in his body. And where there is life, there is hope. When things seem to be at their worst, don't you know God is able to change that?

Rev. Dr. James D. Peters, Jr.

In this, Job made a serious spiritual mistake. True things were very bad. His very ceiling had indeed fallen in and the bottom had fallen out. He seemed to forget that no matter how bad things are, God is still in charge. God is still the author and finisher of our faith. God is still the one who can make a way out of no way. When you are about to give up and think you want to die and everything is hopeless, and there is no way to make it, God is still God.

James Russell Lowell put it this way:

Careless seems the great Avenger; History's pages but record
One death-grapple in the darkness 'twixt old systems and the Word;
Truth forever on the scaffold, wrong forever on the throne,
Yet that scaffold sways the future, and, behind the dim unknown,
Standeth God within the shadow, keeping watch above his own.

If Job had been able, at this moment, to calmly trust himself and his future to God, it is certain that he would not have longed for or wished for death. He would have reasoned that neither the miseries of life nor the perplexities of his pain were a sufficient reason for him to ask God to cancel the gift of life. We have a right to ask God for deliverance from any trouble. Nothing is too big, too much to ask help from God. No person can try to insist that our faith gives us an exemption from any trouble. It is possible for any of us at any time, and all of us at some time, to suffer from physical or emotional situations. But, deeply imbedded in us is a strong belief that a better day is coming. The wicked will cease from troubling. The bible says that "There will be no pain, no night, no sorrow, no crying, no sea and no death in heaven." If you ever find yourself thinking of taking your own life, call someone right away, someone who will pray with you and talk to you, someone who can talk to you about the God who can and will answer prayer. Don't

24

give up. Don't surrender. Just listen to the words of this old, familiar gospel song:

If you will have a little talk with Jesus.
And you can, tell Him all about your troubles.
He will hear your humble cry, and He will answer by and by.
You will feel a little prayer wheel turning,
And you will know that a fire is burning.
Just a little talk with Jesus, makes it right.

III. Those Who Would Choose Life

1.   There are many things which you can say to yourself and to your friends who want reasons to go on living. There are good, strong reasons in favor of being alive. Yes, there are good days, high moments, healthy hours, good times in life. Let me remind you that the powers which we have as human beings, though imperfect, are capable of divine improvement. We all need to remember, when it seems that life is not worth living that, whether long or short, being alive is a gift of God. Being alive gives us a chance to demonstrate the fruit of faith found in the fruit of the spirit.

2.   Do you know that people who are very very sick, and even in comas, expected to die at any moment, can often hear what you say around their bedside. I caution people, in times of critical illness, not to talk about death, because they may be able to hear you. Many times I have been told by people who came out of comas, that my voice in prayer had broken through the coma. So despite what hospitals call comatose, be careful that you don't give up on your loved ones. Every serious, terrible illness does not always lead to death. Don't let anybody try to count God out. Don't give up on God. Miracles do happen.

Have you ever seen one of those miraculous plays in football? Every now and then, with the clock down to zero, and the quarterback fades back to throw a 'Hail Mary' pass into the end zone. It does not happen often, but every now and then somebody on his team catches the pass that wins the game.

You can't give up on life, just when some scientist is about to find a cure for cancer, or Lou Gehrig's disease, or Multiple Sclerosis, or Parkinson's Disease or Autism. The Lord may be about to perform a miracle in your situation. Do you write God off? No. You trust and never doubt. Where there is life, there is hope.

Conclusion

So would you rather be dead than alive? Is that the eternal question with which you are dealing?

Let me ask you "Have you ever been in love?" And if you have, have you ever been heartbroken? In life, sometimes they seem to go together. Well, in the midst of your heartbreak, did you feel that the joy and pleasure of being in love is not worth the pain of being heartbroken? You might have felt that you wanted to die during the period of misery from the pain of the heartbreak. But the poet said. "It is better to have loved and lost, than to never have loved at all." I agree with the poet. For if you ever found love again, weren't you glad you didn't die the first time. For if you are dead, there is no second chance at happiness. And so it is in all areas of life. In spite of all of the miseries of human life, it is better to have been born, than to have never existed. In spite of the shortness, the terrible brevity and imperfections of life, it is worth living. Because of all its hardships and sorrows, we should remember that God almighty is both the author and finisher of life—the Alpha and the Omega, the beginning and the ending of it all.

I must say that, if you believe in it, it's so good to know that there is hope for life after death. It's good to know that when the trials of this life are really over, God has a better place. It's good to know that there is a place where the wicked shall no longer trouble us, and the weary shall be at rest. But, don't rush it. Don't commit suicide!

A hymn by Thomas Dorsey says it this way:

When I've done the best I can, If my friends don't understand,
Then my Lord will carry me Home. After I have done my best,
I will find a peaceful rest, When my Savior carries me home.

Many griefs and sorrows I have witnessed on my part,
On that bright tomorrow, He will mend and heal my wounded heart,
When the best I've done for Thee, Then the best comes back to me
When my Savior carries me Home.

When I've done the best I can, And I'm near the Promised Land,
Then my Lord will carry me Home. When my best I've tried to live,
My mistakes He will forgive, When my Savior carries me Home.

When my day is over and the evening shadows fall,
Faith will cross me over, When I hear my Master sweetly call,
In my friends the best I see, May they see the best in me,
When my Savior carries me Home.

And finally, words paraphrased from the song "Bye and Bye":

Home, Where everyday will be Sunday.
Home, where the wicked will cease from troubling.
Home. Home. Home. Where God is.
Where peace is always around.

WHEN YOU ARE IN A STRAIT-JACKET
Sermon 4: "Is It Normal To Be Impatient?"
By Rev. Dr. James D. Peters, Jr.

"Your words have upheld him who was stumbling, and you have made firm the feeble knees. But now it has come to you, and you are impatient; it touches you, and you are dismayed." (Job 4:4-5 RSV)

As we walk through the book of Job, we find here in Chapter four, the beginning of a number of debates. Words from the friends of Job, and responses and comments from Job, last through much of this great book. The first to speak is Eliphaz. He begins his speech politely. In verse four, his words are a pleasing tribute to Job's reputation, especially in his ability to help others in their difficulties.

For seven days, Eliphaz and his friends had observed a profound silence, being awed and confounded at the sight of Job's unprecedented affliction. Since they had now fully taken in the extent of his illness and having felt the full impact of his bitter complaint, this man forgets that he has come as a friend and a comforter. He begins to reprove, to correct Job.

The sympathetic silence of the friends of Job is now broken by, at first sympathetic, and then unsympathetic speech. Job's desperate words, although not addressed to the friends, demand our attention. They have heard the agony of Job which hung like a heavy cloud over the silence of their visitation. They listen in stark unbelief to the profound cursing which reflected the deep bitterness which Job felt.

Right from the start, there is the insinuation that Job is unable to apply to himself what he preached to others. The words 'impatient' and 'dismayed' also say simply that he was in [what I call] an emotional strait-jacket. The Bible tells the words of Eliphaz, but it does not tell us the tone which he used in making these remarks. Some commentators have found them to be smug, sarcastic and hypocritical. To be sure, they were accusatory. "Even as I have seen, Those who plow iniquity, And sow trouble, reap the same. By the blast of God they perish, And by the breath of His anger they are consumed." (Job 4: 8-9 NKJV)

However, sometimes even when trying to help people in trouble, there is often a danger in being too blunt. Eliphaz might have softened it a bit to say, "Now Job I've got to talk to you about all of this, and you might not like what I have to say. It won't be pleasant, but I must do it." He still would then go on to chastise Job for trying to comfort others, and not being able to personally take the advice which he has given to others. It is clear, at this point, that Eliphaz is convinced that Job must be guilty of something; that Job is lying or trying to hide his involvement in some terrible sin. Well, is it normal? Can we be expected to be impatient when we are going through the kind of situation which Job faced, or some other kind of situation? That is indeed an important question. I have three points.

I. With These Kinds Of Friends, You Don't Need Enemies

1. There are many tragic things that we can say about some of the murmurings of Job's friends. Some of their words were surely out of place. In many ways, he would have been better off if they had not been with him. But there is some truth in

part of what they say, and there are lessons here which might help us in some way. Many of us are good at knowing how other people should act in certain circumstances. We are good at knowing how they should react to problems, and at how he or she should respond to disaster. But when the shoe is on the other foot, when the storm comes in your life, what then?

There was nothing basically wrong with the intent of Job's friends. Their goal is to turn their suffering friend's thoughts from himself to his God. Some of us do the same thing in our partly religious, partly philosophical attempts to deal with trouble in the lives of our friends. Yet, while much of the dialogue which takes place between Job and his friends has proven essential to this great drama, it was the wrong thing to do in this time of crisis for Job. When you are in deep trouble and your whole world is crumbling around you, you do need and desire comforting from your friends. You don't really want philosophical suggestions about why and how things happened. Job really didn't need his friend to tell him that he was impatient. He was hurting too bad.

When you hurt, you will cry. When you are cut, you will bleed; when you are hit hard, you will fall. Be considerate of where a person is before you put them down. We are all human and subject to pain, sorrow, heartbreak, and yes, even impatience. When you are in a difficult situation and God does not seem to come to your rescue, it is normal to be impatient. It is normal to want to be relieved of your suffering right away.

2. However, we must admit that some of these words were not kind. For, these friends came with words that had to hurt Job in many ways. We might have expected some condemnation of Job's complaint against life and fate and God. But, we are not prepared for some of the words which come to us in the text. In fact, it is a shock to hear Job being called impatient. We have been taught to think that Job and patience go hand in hand. But

are Job and the word impatience synonyms? From our earliest Sunday School lessons, we learned that when you think of the first man, you think of Adam. When you think of the strongest man, you think of Samson. When you think of the wisest man, you think of Solomon. And when you think of the most patient man, you automatically think of Job.

But now the mighty man of God has himself suffered deep distress and the first words from his friends are like these. "You gave good advice to others who were suffering. In fact, many would have fallen had it not been for your comforting words. But now that sorrow has come to you, all of the good advice which you gave to them seems to have gone out of the window. Job, you are impatient."

3. What they were saying was, Job, you have seen many people in affliction and distress and you have given them the advice which was right for their situation. You helped them make it through their sorrow. You helped to strengthen their weak hands and feeble knees. Job, because of your words the despondent have been encouraged and those about to give up, have been convinced that the Lord would make a way somehow. Now, you are the one suffering. Have you forgotten your own advice? You must now be an example of how to suffer. You must practice what you have been preaching.

For now it is your turn to suffer. But, instead of being strong, you faint. Trouble touches you and you are too stunned to face it. You are grieving and you seem ready to give up. You seem to be broken. It strikes you down and you seem to be weary and terribly frightened.

Life is strange. What goes around comes around. Sometimes things come around to us which we never sent around. There are problems that are not of our making. We suffer from things that are not our fault. Things happen to us which we have not caused or deserved. Yet, they happen. It's sometimes easy to tell somebody else how to handle it, but when it's your time to cry, what then?

Eliphaz made an appeal to Job's memory. Do you recall, Job, how you helped others when trouble came? Now you curse and cry and seem to forget the words which you spoke. Why not apply some of the same bandages, which you were willing to suggest to others, to bind your own wounds? Questions about why people suffer are difficult questions to which there are no easy answers. If trouble has not come into your life, if you have never felt that you were between a rock and a hard place, hold on for it may well come in some form. The shoe of agony which has been on someone else's foot may well be on your foot. Then what will you do?

II.   When It's Your Turn To Cry

1.   There is a tone of sarcasm in these words. Remember that Job has been through one terrible nightmare after another. He is surely in a terribly difficult place. Don't forget that none of us can accurately measure the impact of a situation on a particular person. So, if we feel a tendency to rebuke, or condemn some of our friends, even on spiritual matters, let us be kind. When somebody is down and out, don't take that time to beat up on them. When you give spiritual guidance to someone in trouble, don't be so hard, so coarse, so direct with your words that you hurt them in the process. There is a time for tough love and a time for gentle compassion.

It's hard to go through life trying to be superhuman. You think about a man losing all that Job lost, and to still be able to come up saying "The Lord has given, the Lord has taken away, blessed be the name of the Lord." That's super human. It's spiritually right and it is the way we ought to think. But when your child is critically ill or deceased, or when it's your dreams which have been blasted, or when it's your future that has been decimated, it's not easy to say blessed be the name of the Lord.

2.   While Job's faith in God is strong, he still wants some answers. If you are still shocked over Job being called impatient, let me tell you that Job did not claim to be the most patient person in history. Job says "What is my strength, that I should wait? and what is my end that I should be patient." (Job 6:11) And "As for me, is my compliant against man? Why should I not be impatient?" (Job 21:4) It might not sound like Job, but it is. Think about it. Job is not the first, nor will he be the last to find himself unequal to the task of practicing what is being preached.

When the teacher is tested, what then? Job's friends, have come to help. They do not understand the mysteries of human suffering, so they often become accusers of the one they wanted to help. Many of their words are ill advised. But in this case I firmly believe that some of the charges against Job are proper. For, there are some real changes which come about when the teacher is tested.

Job was indeed the man whom God praised. He has in the past been the comforter to many who were in trouble. But, now the teacher is tested. There is a lesson here for all of us, but especially for those who hold positions of leadership in the church or who counsel people in trouble. We, who give advice to others, need to be prepared to take our own medicine. Make no mistake about it. In your own life, you may well have to practice the faith and patience which you have preached to someone else.

People just don't expect doctors to get sick, but they do. They don't expect teachers to have questions which they can't answer, but they do. They don't expect mechanics' automobiles to break down, but they do. In fact, they don't even expect morticians to die, but they do.

3.   People are quick to say, "physician, heal thyself", when it comes to preachers. They do not expect preachers to have problems which they cannot solve, but it does happen. They are quick to comment. "Reverend, if you can tell us how to face storms, when they come in your life, we don't want to hear you whine. Don't show any signs of impatience. Haven't you been telling us that 'They that wait upon the Lord shall renew their strength?'" So when the teacher is tested, everyone is going to look and comment. But, the teacher is human too. So let us not get upset about Job's season of impatience. Rather, let us learn from it.

III.   How Can We Acquire Patience?

1.   The impatience of Job, to which I refer, is not an excuse for you to justify your own impatience. Rather it should be an incentive for you to grow in patience. I have seen this happen to people in days gone by. And if it has happened before, it can happen again. Patience is the power to wait for the light of hope to break through the darkness.

To wait for God to heal your body, your career, your, finances, your romantic life, is an exercise in the practice of patience. Patience is expecting freedom, justice and equality when hope unborn has almost died. Patience is the power to suffer and endure. Don't give up on God. When things go bad, be patient in prosperity and in adversity.

"If you can keep your head", as Kipling said, "when all about you are losing theirs and blaming it on you", then you are spiritually mature. The power to wait is born of faith. Patience is a child of faith.

2.   Ask somebody who knows. There are people who have stood where you stand. Many of them have learned that if you will but wait for it, God never will forget to light His lamp. There are people, who know from experience, that the Lord will make a way somehow. Do you know someone who has wallowed, like Job in the low ground of impatience, but God did lift them out of their despair? How do I know that God will fix your faith? I learned it in the school of experience. God did it for me. There was a time when I did indeed question and doubt God. I used to wonder why God took so long. But, I do not anymore.

I have learned that "They that wait upon the Lord shall renew their strength. They shall mount up with wings like eagles; they shall run and not get weary, They shall walk and not faint." (Isaiah 40:31) Sometimes life's journey of faith is one day at a time. God can give us enough faith, love, trust and yes, patience for that one day at a time.

Conclusion

In a song written by Rev. W. C. Martin and Charles Gabriel, they suggest that one who is tempted to be impatient often whispers these words expressing strong faith:

I trust in God, wherever I may be
Upon the land, or on the rolling sea.
For, come what may, from day to day
My heav'nly Father watches over me.

I trust in God, for in the lion's den,
On battlefield, or in the prison pen
Thru praise or blame, Thru flood or flame
My heav'nly father watches over me.

I trust in God, I know He cares for me.
On mountain bleak, or on the stormy sea
Tho' billows roll, He keeps my soul.
My heav'nly Father watches over me.

WHEN YOU ARE IN A STRAIT-JACKET
Sermon 5: "Can You Make a Statement of Faith?"
By Rev. Dr. James D. Peters, Jr.

"For I know that my Redeemer lives, And shall stand at last on the earth; And after my skin is destroyed, this I know, That in my flesh I shall see God: Whom I shall see for myself, and my eyes shall behold, and not another; How my heart yearns within me. (Job 19.25-27 NKJV)

Since the beginning of the existence of human beings on the planet earth, there have been some towering, dramatic statements of faith uttered, or written. Words which can give help to the troubled and hope to those who have lost their hope. These statements of faith have come from the anguish of individuals or the collective wisdom of many. They have been great jewels of inspiration to those impoverished in spirit and great lanterns to light up the often dark pathways of life.

The Apostles' Creed (1.) is a great testimony of faith and a gem of wisdom. Many who are believers in Jesus Christ respect its concepts and conclusions. We have great statements of faith in some of the words of great poetry. For example, these words written during the Korean War in 1953 by Drake, Graham, Shurl and Stillman, was a long-time best-selling record by

Frankie Laine, but then became even more famous when recorded by the great Mahalia Jackson:

> *I believe for every drop of rain that falls, a flower grows.*
> *I believe that somewhere in the darkest night, a candle glows.*
> *I believe for everyone one who goes astray, someone will come, to show the way.*
> *I believe.*
>
> *I believe above the storm the smallest prayer will still be heard.*
> *I believe that someone in the great somewhere hears every word. Every time I hear a new born baby cry, or touch a leaf, or see the sky. Then I know why—*
> *I believe.*

No doubt about it, this poetry is a great pronouncement of faith.

But, I submit to you, that I sincerely believe that in this great poetic book of Job, we have here a marvelous statement of faith. And, it's not a surprise that, it comes with the background of suffering and human frailty. Against the backdrop of the darkest of nights, Job sees the brightest of lights. He makes the most startling discovery of which the human mind is capable. He makes the most astounding pronouncement, the most gripping statement of faith and trust in God possible. He is somehow lifted above the level of the ordinary, far beyond the levels of his own understanding. But, this is what God will do for you if you search for God and stay with God, even in your strait-jacket kinds of situations.

His statement starts off with, "for I know". To simply say, "I hope", I guess may be comfortable for some people. But to reach the depths of faith, there must be some "I knows". "Ifs" and "Maybes" just won't do it. Job uses "I" and "my" three times in verses 26 and 27. There come times when you know that you know that you know, even if you cannot understand what life is doing to you.

Let us examine your and my own personal testimonies of faith. I repeat the question: "Can you make a statement of faith?" I have two points.

I. Our Need For A Suitable Redeemer

1.   We know what Job has been through. We see him sitting in ashes in the city dump having lost everything—material, social and physical which he had enjoyed. Yet, he can talk about a redeemer, a vindicator. It may be coming. He awaits his final judgment. He reminds his friends that, "while I am accused now, I know that I am not guilty. I have maintained my integrity and I look forward to the day of my vindication." Then he makes a noble boast in his confidence in divine justification. And this is one of the great utterances of faith. "I know that my redeemer lives."

Let me share some biblical history and law. In the ancient law, there were strict rules governing who could be a redeemer. In Leviticus beginning in 25:23-45, it spelled out who could redeem property, or persons sold into slavery. There were three conditions. The redeemer or avenger or vindicator had to be firstly, kin to the subject; secondly, willing to act as a redeemer; and thirdly, worthy or able to pay the price of redemption. Redemption was a critical issue and not just anyone could do it. The focus is on a kinsman redeemer.

2.   That is why, that in the book of Revelations there is so much emphasis on whether or not Jesus was worthy to open the book of the seven seals, and thus redeem mankind from the scourge of sin. He had to be kin to humanity, and he was. He was born of the Virgin Mary. He was kin to Israel, being of the root and offspring of David. He had to be willing. You

could not force anyone to redeem someone. They had to do it voluntarily. You remember when they came to Jesus in the garden, and Peter pulled his sword. Jesus said, "if I needed swords, my Father would send 12 thousand angels to fight for me. I give up my life voluntarily". And He had to be worthy or able to redeem. And Jesus was. The cry of Revelation was, "thou art worthy . . . for You were slain, and have redeemed us to God by Your blood." (Rev. 5:9b)

3. Another thing which you need to understand, that adds to the greatness of this statement of Job, is this. The book of Job is among the earliest writings of scripture. By all critical standards, its authorship is ancient. For example, there is no reference to the deliverance of the children of Israel out of slavery in Egypt, and of God holding back the rushing water of the Red Sea. The historical references point to times before the Exodus, before the giving of the law on Sinai.

Rev. Charles Haddon Spurgeon in a sermon from his book entitled "Christ in the Old Testament" focuses on the use of the words "My Redeemer" by Job. (2.) It points to this passage as one of the references to Christ in the O.T. because Job lived along way back in biblical history. It was written before Isaiah said, "A virgin shall be with child". Before he said, "His name shall be called wonderful counselor, mighty God. Everlasting Father, Prince of Peace." It was written way back, before Daniel saw God as a stone hewn out of the mountain; before Ezekiel saw God as a wheel in the middle of a wheel. Way back in the early, early days, perhaps without scripture to guide him, Job has a vision of the eternal redeemer, Jesus Christ, saying, "I know that my redeemer lives."

We who live today have so much more to work with. We have so much more history and law and poetry and gospel, even the letters of the Apostle Paul. If Job could see, and declare, and believe in the eternal Redeemer, with so little to guide him, we can surely develop our own deep statements of faith.

II.   Faith Sees God Dramatically Alive.

1.   Job's faith is in the resurrection of the dead. It is not in his present human body, so frail, so likely to be torn with pain, consumed with sickness even destroyed by worms. His faith is in a new body. He says, "skin worms shall destroy this body, yet in my flesh will I see God." Job sees a spiritual body which will be free from corruption.

While Job does not understand what life is doing to him at this point, now, he believes that he will ultimately be vindicated. He wanted to have his name cleared. He wanted his friends to stop urging him to confess his sin. But we who live on this side of Calvary, who are blessed not to live in B.C. days but in A.D. days, know that our redeemer will not only vindicate the innocent, and forgive the guilty, but will also save them from their sins. What a great vision Job had! What a statement of faith he delivered. We who live today are excited that he could see that far down the line of time.

2.   Do you sense what has probably happened to Job? Sorrow has given him marvelous power of spiritual intuition. It has trained him to trust. In times of trouble many people are able to develop enlarged visions of the power of God. A hymn writer said, "In the furnace God will prove you, thus to bring you forth more bright." When it's dark, when trouble comes in your life, oftentimes your spiritual vision will be improved. Many will see more than they have ever seen.

Once, as a city boy wandering in the unfamiliar and frightening darkness of a rural country road, I faced a frightening moment. In the dark wilderness my only friend was my flashlight, to keep me on the winding trail to get back to the camp. Suddenly my flashlight, died on me. The meandering trail which I was to follow was gone, and with no flashlight, it seemed so very far from where I needed to be. Why did I, a city boy, venture alone into this deep darkness where I could not see my hand in front of my face? Hopelessly I clung to a small tree and wished for some light from somewhere.

Suddenly, a flash from a lightning bolt flashed across the horizon. And in that fleeting moment I could see the path again. I could only see far enough to note the direction of the trail. That one flash of light, started me on my way. That one great light made me know where the small hill was, beyond which was the light of my camp and my way back.

3.   That, in a much larger sense, is what I believe happened to Job. He was alienated from health and happiness; from friends and family, and when it seemed that even God had turned his back on him. In a moment of deep darkness and total despair, suddenly, a flash of the light of divine revelation came to him. It lit up the dark sky of his dilemma and showed him a vision which made him know his Redeemer lived. And in the afterglow of that one vision for that moment, he came out of the darkness into a marvelous light. Now, he could give this very personal testimony, this bold statement of faith: I know that my redeemer lives.

He is not saying that his redeemer shall live. He is not saying that his redeemer did live. He said, ". . . my redeemer lives". He lives yesterday, today and forever.

The song writer picked it up and said:

> *Because he lives I can face tomorrow;*
> *Because he lives all fear is gone*
> *Because I know he holds the future, and*
> *Life is worth the living just because he lives.*

Conclusion

Job gets flamboyant with his statement, with his praise. He goes on to say, "Whom I shall see for myself". Think about it. He does not expect to see God by proxy or to understand him through an interpreter. No. He says, "I shall see him for myself." At this time human beings did not have a clear concept of a personal god. Job, like others, did not know that he could have a personal relationship with God which would cause him to declare: "I know that my redeemer lives."

This matter of faith must be based on a personal knowledge of God. When you talk about God, you must be able to say "my God". You must have a personal knowledge of God for yourself.

If you want to make you own declaration of faith, this must be one of the components. Can you talk about "your God"? Can you look forward to the return of "your Savior"? Do you believe that you will see him one day? That He shall stand? If so, you, like Job, are on your way to being able to make a real, "statement of faith".

Listen to the words of songwriter Alfred Ackley. Notice how personal he gets.

I serve a risen Savior, He's in the world today.
I know that he is living, whatever men may say
I see his hand of mercy, I hear his voice of cheer.
And just the time I need him, He's always near.

He lives, he lives, Christ Jesus lives today!
He walks with me and talks with me Along life's narrow way.
He lives, He lives salvation to impart.
You ask me how I know he lives, he lives within my heart.

Will you make your statement like Job's? Do you have your own testimony? Are you able to make your own statement of faith? Does it meet the test of difficult days? Do you have a testimony? Can you make your own statement of faith?

One man said about his own conversion, "I said I wasn't going to tell nobody, but I couldn't keep it to myself."

(1.) The basic creed of Reformed churches, as most familiarly known, is called the Apostles' Creed. It has received this title because of its great antiquity; and because it dates from very early times in the Church, a half century or so from the last writings of the New Testament.

(2.) Rev. Charles Haddon Spurgeon, who lived from 1834 to 1892 and served as pastor of the Metropolitan Tabernacle Church London, said in the book, "Christ in the Old Testament." The sermon title is "I know that my Redeemer liveth." pages 479-to-490. "What good is honey in the wood to me, if I like the fainting Israelites, dare not eat. It is honey in my hand, honey on my lip, which enlightens mine eyes like those of Jonathan. What is gold in a mine to me. It is the gold in my purse which will satisfy my necessities, purchasing the bread I need. So, what is a kinsman if he be not a kinsman to me. A Redeemer who does not redeem me, an avenger who will never stand for my blood, of what avail were such? But Job's faith was strong and firm in the conviction that the Redeemer was his.

WHEN YOU ARE IN A STRAIT-JACKET
Sermon 6: "Crying Over Spilled Milk"
By Rev. Dr. James D. Peters, Jr.

"Oh, that I were as in months past, As in the days when God watched over me; When His lamp shone upon my head, And when by His light I walked through darkness; Just as I was in the days of my prime, When the friendly counsel of God was over my tent;" (Job 29:2-4 NKJV)

Here is the cry of a man who is moved to tears over the unpredictable circumstances and situations in which he finds himself. Why, if he could go back just a few days, weeks, months, things would be much better. He is lamenting, he is weeping, he is regretting, he is fretting, yes he is crying over spilled milk. This man is known throughout history as a man of great patience. But, here he is crying about how glorious his yesterdays were, and how miserable his today is.

When tragedy came to Job's life, it took many forms. The test points to many as a form of regret. In this message we look at Job's material losses. For in spite of his total losses he also suffered great material losses, health reverses and the loss of his social status.

We don't take these losses lightly. When you work hard, you deserve some of the finer things of life. When you labor for some of life's comforts, it is a cruel blow to have them taken away. Or, whether it is done by some thief who breaks into your home; or by some smooth-talking, white-collar-criminal who gets you to sign away your possessions through some cunning trickery; or, whether by some unknown and unpredictable circumstance over which you have no control, it's difficult to lose material possessions.

Other concerns may be: when your health becomes a matter of concern and then you have to watch what you eat—or when the agony of the diagnosis or the uncertainties of the prognosis leave you wondering—or, when there is no mistake that what you face is really serious, permanent and will restrict your activities for the rest of your life—when surgery looms over your head, or worse, when there is no surgery that can solve your health problems! It's rough. It's painful to hear over and over that medicine is an inexact science. And it seems that you hear from the lips of a sick person these words "When you've got your health and strength, you've got everything."

When your reputation is damaged by the pain of public embarrassment—When the social position which you worked so hard to achieve, is threatened, or put down by some personal problem or set of circumstances, it's rough. It shakes the best of us to our very depths. It makes us think. You know what happened to Job.

So, in a time of deep trouble, or painful sickness, or the loss of family and wealth and prestige, it is not surprising to hear Job cry out for a return to yesterday, or to utter words of depressing regret. It is not surprising to look backward, while in this terrible strait-jacket situation, and cry over spilled milk.

What lessons can we learn by listening to Job's cry, as we look at our own responses to tragedy, and trying to profit from it? I have two points.

I. Why Do We Cry Over Spilled Milk?

1. Some of us cry over spilled milk in a conscious or unconscious effort to duck the danger which we face. We want to go back to the time when the battles and heartaches were the responsibility of someone else. How easy it would be to be able to go back to when your parents carried the weight. Many people want to go back to some distant day because they tend to idealize the past, making it seem better than it was. Haven't you known people who did that? The children of Israel were like that. As slaves in Egypt, they could not have been in more terrible conditions. But, when Moses led them away from bondage, they found no thrill in looking forward. Instead, some forgot the agony of making brick without straw. They realized that Moses had a vision of the future, so some of them wanted to choose another leader and go back to Egypt. It is not surprising that not one of these renegades reached the Promised Land. In order to reach life's "promised land", you must have a "promised land" mentality. And wishing you were back in Egypt, or back to the conditions which you once knew, is not the way to do it.

2. But Job's longing was more reasonable and more excusable than any of these which I have mentioned. His desire to turn back the clock, his wish to be as he was, had its birth in a desire to escape the terrible tragedy which had come upon him. He had lost the joy of a once happy home. He had lost his material wealth and his abundant health. Things are bad. Pain has become his constant companion. In many ways, his life is without meaning. He feels that he has changed from a glowing asset to a terrible liability. Yes, some of us can at least understand why he cries out, "Oh, that I were as in the months of old." We can almost forgive him for crying over spilled milk. Strait-jackets hurt. They make you wish for a return to the yesterday when there was no strait-jacket, at least, not the one you face now.

3. It is a waste of time to cry over spilled milk because nothing can change yesterday. What is spilled is spilled. To wish that you were as in months past is not possible, period. Some people go through life refusing to accept the inevitable. We might not like the law of gravity, but it is still the law. It won't change just because we don't like it. If we ignore it, we can break some bones. Crying will give you red eyes at night and a headache in the morning. But it won't change anything.

And, it does not help to try to place the blame for the spilled milk of your circumstances. It does not matter who spilled it, it is still spilled. Some cry, "I do not deserve this. This is not fair. It was not my fault."

But, the milk is still spilled. The strait-jacket situation still exists. "Whose fault is this? Or who did sin and who must pay?" These are not appropriate questions for spiritually attuned people. For judges and courts and juries, yes they are, but not for you. You don't need to know why. You are a child of God. You are trusting in the Supreme Power who made the world. You are leaning on the God who holds tomorrow. You should not be crying over yesterday.

4. Not many of the hymns and gospel songs even focus on bygone days. But the romantic ballads and musing poets have much to say about the temptation to, and danger of, spending your time crying over spilled milk. And why not, you may ask? For often, it is in the areas of our romantic adventures or misadventures that we are likely to have our most painful regrets. Allow me to quote as much as I can remember of a portion of "Looking Back", a hugely popular, romantic song by the late, great Nat King Cole from back in the fifties, and Brook Benton in the sixties:

Looking back over my life,
I see love turned to strife

But I know, oh yes I know,
I'd never make that same mistake again.

Once my cup was overflowing,
But I gave nothing in return
Now I can't begin to tell you,
What a lesson I have learned.

Are you familiar with the book of poetry entitled **_The Rubaiyat_**, written in the year 1120? In his musings, Omar Khayyam wrote #71, words which you may hear at funerals:

The Moving Finger writes; and, having writ,
Moves on: nor all your Piety nor Wit.
Shall lure it back to cancel half a line,
Nor all your Tears wash out a Word of it.

Well, what is he saying? It is that all of your piety, your love for, and service to God, that all your wisdom, no matter how extensive your training, shall lure back yesterday to change it one iota. Neither will all your tears, we're talking about crying over spilled milk, wash out a word of it. Lord, help us.

What is written is written. What is done is done. Yesterday is gone, Job. You, who are crying out your heart every night over something which is past and gone, let it go. A familiar gospel song says:

Time is filled with swift transition
Naught of earth unmoved can stand.
Build your hopes on things eternal
Hold to God's unchanging hand.

(words and music written by Jennie Wilson and F. L. Eiland)

II.   How Can We Stop Crying Over Spilled Milk?

1.   We must find a way. Why—Because if we spend our time crying over yesterday, we will lose out on today and that would be a fatal mistake. Because if we lose today, we lose all we have. Today is the hinge on which all of tomorrow hangs. The Bible says, "This is the day which the Lord has made; let us rejoice and be glad in it." (Psalm 118:24) If you face your future feeling blessed to be alive now and thanking God for today, the word of God has found a place in your heart. Don't spend your time crying over yesterday until you mess up your today. Don't go through life praising the beauties of yesterday until you can't see anything of value today. Looking back, crying over spilled milk is human and almost everybody does it. But, it has no power to change yesterday, and it can do real damage to your today and your tomorrow.

In another old popular song, Dionne Warwick sang:

A fool would lose tomorrow looking back at yesterday.

In a great traditional, gospel song with a lasting message for today and tomorrow the author says:

I don't know about tomorrow, I just live from day to day.
I don't borrow from its sunshine, For its skies may turn to gray
I don't worry o'er the future. For I know what Jesus said,
And today I'll walk beside Him, For he knows what is ahead.
Many things about tomorrow, I don't seem to understand
But I know who holds tomorrow, And I know who holds my hand.

2.   How can we avoid crying over spilled milk? Well, we have a better chance than Job. Job had many things, but, since this is one of the earliest of Bible writings, we don't know how

much sacred scripture Job had before him. We have the Old Testament <u>and</u> the New Testament.

Because you see, we can stand on the shoulders not only of Job, and the patriarchs of the Old Testament, but also on the shoulders of the Apostle Paul in the New Testament.

We have the blessing of the fact that a man named Paul wrote a letter from jail to the church at Phillipi. Please read what he said in the third Chapter of Phillipians, dealing with the subject of looking back and crying over spilled milk. He talks about some of the problems of his past. He brags about being circumcised the 8th day of the tribe of Benjamin. He talks about a zeal which drove him to persecute the church. But, he said, "I made all of those things secondary to my primary goal. That I might know Him and the power of his resurrection." And then in verse 13, he says "but, this one thing I do. Forgetting those things which are behind, [Oh yes, I am on my subject, so I'll repeat that phrase.] Forgetting those things which are behind, And reaching forth to those things which are before [I won't spend any time crying over spilled milk, but] I press toward the mark for the prize of the high calling of God in Christ Jesus."

3.   You see, sometimes we, like Job, spend so much time crying over what we have lost, we forget what we have left. That's what we do concerning handicapped persons when we focus on the wrong thing. Just because someone is challenged in sight, in hearing, in walking or in some other way, we tend to see what is missing and seem to forget that what counts is what is left. Job is crying so much about what has happened to him, that, for a moment, he forgets that he still has God. He still has God. He has lost a lot, but he has not lost everything.

If you possess God, if you are on speaking terms with God, you have the possibility to survive. Then, that is all you really need. Think about it, you have the power to become a child of God. It is true now, and always will be so. All you need is God. With God, all things are possible.

God will allow you come out of yourself. Excruciating pain is terrible. It tends to demand your complete attention. But if you get caught up in helping somebody else through their pain, it will ease some your own. Tears may wet your face from morning to night. But find somebody else with a tear-stained face, to help them, and God will dry your tears. If your heart is broken and bleeding go out and try to bind up the brokenhearted. If you have known God, He can change the message of your tears to make them a road map to new joy. Don't you know God is able?

Conclusion

You see, you can regain what you have lost. Yes, it hurts to lose personal possessions, cars, houses, furs, jewelry, stocks and bonds. But, do you remember the widow who gave the last bit of her flour and oil to feed the preacher man? God had, and still has an empty oil cruse refill program. God will make up for the shortages in your life. Even if you think you have lost everything, as the old preachers used to say, God owns the cattle on a thousand hills. God has a restoration program. God has a program for making up the shortage program. God has an "I will give you more than you lost program." If your life is on the down side, God can change it to being on the up side.

God gave Job more than he had before. But, that's another sermon. But in telling Bible stories, there is no real mystery. You have read the story of Job. You already know that in the end of Job's strait-jacket situation, God gave him more than he had lost. You know what God has done and can do for you. Didn't God make a way out of no way for you in other times when you have been in trouble? Didn't God open doors for you that no one could close? Have you forgotten what God did for you? Cry sometimes if you must, but stop crying over spilled milk. Better still, sing this rich and uplifting song:

Like a ship that's tossed and driven,
Battered by an angry sea.
When the storms of life are raging,
And their fury falls on me.

I wonder what I have done
That makes this race so hard to run.
Then I say to my soul, take courage,
The Lord will make a way, Somehow.

He's a friend to the friendless. He's a mother to the motherless. He's a father to the fatherless. He's my joy in times of sorrow. He's my hope for tomorrow. Surely, surely, surely, don't you know? God is able.

WHEN YOU ARE IN A STRAIT-JACKET
Sermon 7: "Turning Back the Hands of Time"
By James D. Peters, Jr.

"Oh that I were as in months past, as in the days when God watched over me; When His lamp shone upon my head, and when by His light I walked through darkness;" (Job 29.2-3 NKJV)

Here is the cry of a man who is unhappy with his present condition and who longs for things to be like they were in the past. His wail is human, his regret floods the air. His cry is hauntingly familiar. For, so many of us have uttered the same cry. We tend to frame our regrets about our present condition by wishing, praying, desiring, that things were like they used to be. We think about days which are past and gone and remember only the good things about them. We dare to say, to our friends, to ourselves . . . . and even to God, that we wish we could, turn back the hands of time.

In Chapter 29, verse 2 we find Job's final speech. It begins with these words framed by memories of his place in society. Job now wishes for better days, days which were his, just a short time ago. He contrasts his present with his past. He thinks about the difference in his condition during his good days and his present condition. And, make no mistake about it, Job had lost a lot. His life had suddenly changed from a seemingly never-ending noonday to a seemingly eternal midnight. What would you do if it happened to you? Think about it.

Job's review of his life is a most important look at the things which were the measure of a person's success in that day. He has been a person respected in his community, loved by his family and feared by his enemies. When persons considered who to invite to a special function, Job was not only invited, but was seated at the head table. When he stood to speak, everybody stopped talking and listened to him.

Job was somebody. His pride in his achievements should not be misunderstood. They were legitimate and not self righteous. He declared that he was eyes to the blind and feet to the lame. And, now he is reduced to a nobody. People who used to seek his advice, now spit on him. From the ash heap of the city dump, with his body covered with sores, with his prestige gone, he is a mere shadow of his former self. No wonder he wants to turn back the hands of time.

At first look, we might think that Job's request is bad. For history ought to have taught us that, no matter how much you want to, you can't turn back the clock. If Job is crying because of what people are saying about him or thinking about him, we can see the folly of his cry. [For, though most of us have done it too, we all know that crying about what people say about you won't stop them from talking.] But, if we look closely at the text we find that the focus of his complaint seems to be on his spiritual losses. No doubt about it, any person who had experienced such great reverses would be filled with regret. And, when those losses are spiritual, if his reference is to the condition of his heart and soul, than we can begin to understand and agree with the depth of his pain. You see, his soul was depressed and his regrets were bitter. He felt that he had lost the light of God's face. His joy in the Lord was at a low ebb, and he regretted this. His cry makes sense to him at this point. There are many times when looking back can bring painful memories. Job's sorrow was remembering his former life which was so full and happy. No wonder he cries, "Oh that I were as in months past, as in the days when God preserved me." (Job 29:2 KJV) He wanted to turn back the hands of time, to somehow escape from his present condition.

Job had to feel the sting of both the material losses and the spiritual losses. This sermon deals with the spiritual losses. But, rather than focus on Job, let us take a good look at ourselves. Let us examine areas where we may be feeling the same kind of pain which Job felt. Let us see if we too want to turn back the hands of time.

And let us determine whether you or anyone can, by looking back, really be successful in, "Turning Back the Hands of Time". I have two points.

I. Why Spiritual Losses Ought to Bring Bitter Regrets

1.   To lose anything is bad. But to lose that which is part of your spiritual makeup, is both a tragic and troublesome loss. You see it is a great thing for a person to be near God. It is choice privilege to be admitted into the inner circle of fellowship and to know that God is your heavenly Father. And, so often, you don't know what you had until you have lost it. For there is no darkness like the darkness which falls on the eyes, that are accustomed to the light. No one is as spiritually bankrupt as the one who has been spiritually rich. The person, who has never really known God, cannot imagine what it must be like to lose communication with God. The things which Job cries about losing, in the words of this text, are not simple things. He is crying about major losses, and wishing that he could turn back the hands of time, so that he might have them back again.

2.   First he complains that he has lost the power of divine preservation. He says, "'Oh that I were as in months past, as in the days when God preserved me." (Job 29:2 KJV) God will preserve you. There are times you can feel God building a fence around you to keep your enemies away from you. There are times when you know that God will do as He promised—to give His angels charge over you, lest you dash your foot against a stone. If you lose that, you have lost something vital. Think about facing every day without protection, without being able to whisper in times of trouble. "The Lord is my light and my salvation, whom shall I fear?" (Psalm 27:1 KJV) Or, "I will say of the Lord, he is my refuge and my fortress, my God, in him will I trust." (Psalm 91:2 KJV) If you can't say that, you are in trouble.

Job also felt that he has lost Divine Consolation. He wants to turn back the hands of time to when God's light shone upon his head—To the time when God's sun was at its noonday height—To when he rejoiced without ceasing and triumphed from morning to night in the God of his salvation. Who, that has known the joy of the Lord, can be content after having lost it? What would you do if this happened to you? I suggest that you would cry out like Job.

Job also felt that he had lost Divine Illumination. "By his light" he says, "I walked through darkness". That is to say, he has seen dark days before, but God was always with him to light up every dark valley. You can't beat walking with God. Proverbs tells us, "He is as wise as Solomon who walks with God, but he is a fool who trusts to his own understanding". You cannot light your own pathway. If you can't have the light of the Lord, you are surely lost. Whether you try to do things which are complicated or simple, you need the light of the Lord. If you don't have it, you are in trouble.

3. Job also felt he had lost Divine Communion. There is a need for divine communion. For every human being needs to have blessed fellowship with the divine creator. "He who dwells in the secret place of the Most High high shall abide under the shadow of the Almighty." (Psalm 91:1 KJV) That person is blessed indeed. And anyone who has known that blessing fellowship and lost it is in big trouble. It would be better if you were rich and lost all your money; better if you were healthy, and now are bedridden; better if you were famous, and lost your popularity. No loss can equal the loss of communion with God. No eclipse is so complete as that which blots out the face of God in your life. No storm is so severe as the one which shakes you till you cannot feel the presence of God. No wonder Job cries out for days gone by. He has every reason to want to sing, the words of that old hymn . . .

Where is the blessedness I knew, when first I saw the Lord?
Where is the soul refreshing view of Jesus and his word?

Under these conditions, who wouldn't want to sing . . .

Take me back, take me back . . . to the place where I first believed . . .

He wanted to get out of his terrible situation. He wanted to turn back the hands of time.

II. Are You Less Spiritual Than You Used To Be?

1. What a deep, probing, and personal question to ask. Who would want to say yes? Who would admit to such a condition? But, here the question is before us. And since you don't have to answer aloud, but in the quiet of your own heart, answer to yourself. Are you less spiritual than you used to be? Have you deteriorated in grace? Have you decayed in spirit? Have you been back-sliding into bad habits? Have you declined in

the faith? Do you need to turn back the hands of time in your search for and service to God?

Well, let me ask you where you think you really stand spiritually? You do understand the plain words of Micah 6.8 (NKJV): "What does the Lord require of you, but to do justly, and to love mercy and to walk humbly with your God?" Are you doing it? Is there any humility in what you do? I see a lot of haughtiness. I see too many people with stuck up attitudes. I see too many people acting like they are better than somebody else. Where is your humility? Some of you used to have it, didn't you? But now, even in our places of worship, too many of us tend to think more of ourselves than we ought to.

Were you once offended by things which don't bother you now? Once you despised anything which looked like it was illegal or unlawful. Are you more receptive to that which is immoral? Were you once cautious about your language? But now, do you curse or say negative things about people without thinking? Has your ability to love your enemies increased or decreased? Oh, think about how you used to be. Is there a difference now? Are you less, spiritually, than you used to be?

2.   How are you when it comes to your devotional habits? What about private prayer? Didn't you used to pray on a regular basis? There was a time when many of us couldn't get up in the morning until we thanked God that our bed was not a cooling board . . . and our cover was not a winding sheet. Some people would find a moment at lunch time to whisper a word of thanks to God. And before you went to bed at night, you would kneel beside your bed, and say a word of thanks to God. But, now, what do you do? Are you in too much of a hurry in the morning? Too ashamed at noontime and too tired at night to stop and pray? That after all that God has done for you, do you think you ought to regret acting like that? You ought to want to turn back the hands of time.

3.   And your zeal for the Lord, where is it? Do you get excited about being able to come to church? Do the great hymns of faith ignite the flame of your faith? Do the words and melody of some gospel songs keep you humming all through the week? Do you still feel joy bells ringing in your heart when someone lifts a prayer to God? Why not? What is wrong? God has not changed. Oh, you left where you grew up. Did that make a difference? God is still God. When is the last time you invited someone to church, or to your place of worship? Are you involved with any community charity or some program to help those less fortunate than yourself? Where is your zeal for spiritual service? What's wrong? You probably did it in days gone by. Times when there were no carpeted floors in church. No thermostats to control the temperature. No fine-tuned grand piano or electric organ or keyboard.

It could be that, if not you, your parents had one Sunday-go-to-meeting suit or dress, and they had no car. However they could, they made it to church every Sunday, and had real excitement about being in the house of the Lord! And now, since life may be better for you than it was for them, have you forgotten what God has done for you? You have more than one suit or dress. Now, you may have two or three cars in the family, with more than a hundred horsepower engines in them, or four wheel drive, or a stick shift car, but you seem to care less. [Or, as the old preachers used to say, have I stopped preaching and gone to meddling?] If that is the case, so be it.

Tell me, are you less, spiritually, than you used to be? And if so, maybe you ought to ask God to turn back the hands of time. So that even in your own personal difficult times, you can know God close up. Yes, even you can be on speaking terms with God.

WHEN YOU ARE IN A STRAIT-JACKET

Conclusion

I have talked about conditions in which you might be justified, like Job, to want to turn back the hands of time. But, that's not really what I am going to suggest as I come to a close. You see, in your dealings with God it won't do you any good to have spiritual regrets, and not do anything about them. If you don't work to change your spiritual condition, you will be the same way a year from now. This is the way it is with spiritual things. Time won't make you better. You have to work on your own situation. Some people get satisfaction out of voicing their regrets; crying about their desire to turn back the hands of time. They say, oh, if I knew back then, what I know now, things would be so very different. Well, what would you do differently? There are no guarantees that you would not still be filled with regrets. How much better would you do if you had it to do all over?

I could turn back the time on my watch, to make it read 6:00 A. M. But, that would not make it be 6:00 A. M. I could change the date on a calendar to January. But, that would not make it January. Never mind trying to use your hands on the clock to turn back the hands of time, change your thinking. Change your mind-set. Let this mind be in you which was also in Christ Jesus. Try to improve spiritually. Thank God that you are still alive.

Yes, in your mind's eye you can daydream about the days when things were like you wanted them to be. But then you come back to reality. When you look at the clock and the calendar, it is still a matter or dealing with right now. When you get through wishing and hoping and begging and pleading for a better day that has gone by, it will still be today on the clock of your circumstances.

So, in the final analysis, trying to turn back the clock is a negative thing which, by itself, won't really help you at all.

Popular romantic songwriters for years have tried to glamorize turning back the clock to yesterday. But, they failed if they stopped with references to days gone by.

Yet, life is filled with good times and bad times: Light and Darkness; Hope and Despair; Joy and Sorrow. The challenge is to face the future in faith without living in the make-believe land of "Turning Back the Hands of Time".

Think about old songs like "Glory to His Name" (lyrics by Elisha A. Hoffman). It might seem to start out talking about <u>yesterday.</u>

> *Down at the cross where my Savior Died.*
> *Down where for cleansing from sin I cried.*
> *There to my heart was the blood applied,*
> *Glory to His name.*

But, it moves to what you can do and feel <u>today</u>.

> *I am so wondrously saved from sin*
> *Jesus so sweetly abides with-in*
> *There at the cross where He took me in*
> *Glory to His name.*

Then it moves to what <u>tomorrow</u> can bring.

> *Come to the fountain so rich and so sweet.*
> *Cast down Thy soul at the Savior's feet*
> *Plunge in today and be made complete*
> *Glory to His Name.*

> *Glory to His name,*
> *Glory to His name,*
> *There to my heart was the blood applied*
> *Glory to His name.*

When You Are In A Strait-Jacket
Sermon 8: "Do You Stand In The Window Of Disappointment?"
By Rev. Dr. James D. Peters, Jr.

"Did not I weep for him who was in trouble? Was not my heart grieved for the poor and needy? But when I looked for good, then evil came to me; and when I waited for light, there came darkness." (Job 30:25-26 AMP)

Have you ever stood, in the quiet of the night, and looked out of the window. You didn't know why you looked or what you were looking for. You didn't expect to see anything different, nor did you want to see anything in particular. But still you looked. Perhaps even, possibly as recently as last night, in your personal strait-jacket type of situation, you stood in the window of disappointment. The house is quiet, the night is dark. The questions are unanswered, but still you look.

There can be no question about it. Job is suffering from terrible sickness. He is in excruciating pain both day and night. In addition to the terrible eruptions of his skin, he had trouble breathing. The constant discharge from his ulcers made his garment filthy. It stiffened as the discharge dried, and clung to his skin. And yet, in the midst of his misery, he gives us a picture of the man he used to be. In this gripping autobiographical moment he tells all who will listen, in his day or in this day, of how he cared for the poor when he was in the bloom of physical and material health. In Chapter 29, verses 12 through 16, Job talks at length about how he treated people. "Because I delivered the poor who cried, the fatherless, and him that had none to help him. The blessing of him who was about to perish came upon me, and I caused the widow's heart to sing for joy. I was eyes to the blind and feet was I to the lame. I was a father to the poor and needy; the cause of him I did not know I searched out." (Job 29:12-13, 15-16 AMP) It was like Job was feeling like saying 'I was not selfish in my wealth. I treated people good. No little child did I injure, no widow did I oppress. Why, then, am I suffering so?'

If you have not heard these kinds of questions from the lips of suffering servants of God, I have. How can the experience of Job help us if we stand in the window of disappointment, when we are in a strait-jacket? I have two points.

I.   Do We Reap What We Sow?

1.   Job outlines his expectations. His present circumstances are as different from what they used to be as darkness is from light. He looked for good, but evil came. Job had never ignored an appeal from the poor. On the basis of the rule, "People reap what they sow" (Gal 6:7c TNIV), Job should be treated as he treated others. But no, his cry seems to be unheard by God. He is ignored by his fellow human beings also. It hurts, when you have been good to people. And worst of all, it seems that his cry was not even heard by God.

Job sounds like so many of us. When we are in a strait-jacket type of situation, we tend to recite and repeat stories of the days when we were well and strong and doing good things. We just feel somehow, that if we have been good to people, that people will be good to us. That if we have spent our time being good to those in trouble, that when we are in trouble life will be good to us. So, when the opposite seems to happen to us, when it seems that even God has forgotten or forsaken us, we feel lost, cheated or deeply disappointed.

Job, here, references his own morality. "I have made a covenant with my eyes. Why should I look at a young woman? (31:1-2) Let me be weighed in a just balance, that God should know my integrity.(31:6) If my heart has been enticed by a woman, Or if I have lurked at my neighbor's door, Then let my wife grind for another, And let others bow down over her. For that would be wickedness; Yes it would be iniquity worthy of judgment." (31: 9-11) Do we reap what we sow?

2.   Do you really care for people who are going through some of life's deep water, wearing, as it were a strait-jacket around their bodies. Let me tell you, if you get a lift from someone else's grief, there is something wrong with you. If we are truly Christians, we must weep with those who weep. When you find joy in someone else's family problems, financial situations, physical or mental sicknesses, or the burden of their bereavements, if this gives you some feeling of power or superiority, there is something terribly wrong with you. The reaping and sowing is God's business. And if you do good for others, God will make it right someday—in His own way and in His own time, not always from the people you have helped, but often from somebody else.

3.   What Job seems to be saying is that he feels that God has an obligation to keep sorrow away from his door since he has been good to people. We tend to want to challenge Job, while we often secretly feel the same way. Job's so-called friends try to say that his premise is wrong. That God is so holy and unimpeachable that we have no right to question God for permitting evil to come into our lives. Their premise may be logical, but the conclusion drawn from it is wrong. Yes, God is our creator. But, it is still possible for evil to break in on us.

Some things which happen to us ought not to happen. We do not deserve many of them. But the conclusion that evil will win out in the end, is wrong. The conclusion that God does not care what happens to us, is also wrong.

I have developed a short recipe. If you follow the recipe, you will wind up with the end product.

Mix in a cup of real faith in the large bowl of your circumstances

Fold in two of your broken dreams

Add three cups of your self-sacrificing love

Add the fluid of own teardrops

Stir with your hand, guided by your broken heart

Bear the heat in the oven of tribulation overnight, and

You will find that joy, comes in the morning.

II.   In The Hour Of Crisis, What Will God Do?

1.   A survey of Job's misery, like yours when you are in a strait-jacket, has much in common. The pain which Job suffered was seemingly continuous, and without interruption. Day and night were no different, morning and evening were all the same. He could not tell Monday from Tuesday. Excruciating pain can almost drive you out of your mind. Have you ever been in that place?

There was the mental anguish which Job suffered. When you have known physical pain, then you compared it to the mental and emotional torture which life can give, which would you choose? If you had a choice, it would often be the physical pain. Anguish can tear you apart. Disobedient children can sap your strength; unappreciative parents can shatter your dreams, loved ones can break your heart.

One of the things which seemed to most keenly lacerate Job's bosom was the feeling that the God whom he had loved and served had forgotten about him. It seemed, in this strait-jacket season of personal disappointment, that God remained deaf to Job's cries. Job felt that God was insensitive to his sorrow. He said, "I cry unto you and you do not hear me. I stand before you and you seem not to see me." When all of your hope is in God, and you don't seem to be able to see God, this can be the most depressing time of your life.

Job cries aloud about his misery. "I have become a brother to the jackals, a comrade to the ostriches, these desert creatures who screech with loud and piercing voices in their pain." (Job 30:29) Then in one reference to musical instruments he gives a tortured description of his woe, saying, "My harp is turned to mourning, and my flute to the voice of those who weep." (Job 30:31)

2.   Job was disappointed in meeting with fearful evils when he was looking for good. Disappointment is one of the inevitable trials of life. How many of our fondest hopes become shattered dreams? Disappointment aggravates trouble. When the eye is adjusted for and expecting to see a bright light, the gloom of a dark place seems darker than a dark country road.

Disappointment sometimes makes us feel that we have been ignorant about who and what God is like. We reason that, either we judged life by what seemed to be and was not, or we trusted too much in unknown things. Disappointment can be discipline. It can sharpen our faith and strengthen our resolve to "make it somehow". We need a stout faith to stand up against the blows of unexpected troubles.

But, let me tell you right now. Disappointment will never destroy the faith of the one who truly trusts in God. You may stand in your window of disappointment, wondering if help is ever coming. But you should rest assured that God will call out to you, pick you up, and turn you around. God will open doors which no one can close.

3.   Ask God questions like Job did, if you want to. God can handle it. Say like Job, if you have to, "was I not good to the poor? Now I must wander in darkness. I must stand in my window in the dark of night, not knowing what the morning will bring." You need to understand that God's morning may not come when the sun comes up. Some nights are long-term nights. But, you can be assured that morning will come. And, you can count on the fact that God will respond to your questions.

Don't you like the way Moses said it at a time when darkness and despair were all around him? That was a time when death and funerals were a daily occasion. Listen to Moses in Psalm 91 giving us and the children of Israel some instructions on how to survive, some methods of survival. I know you want to survive, so read this.

"I will say of the Lord, He is my refuge and my fortress; My God; in Him will I trust. Surely He shall deliver you from the snare of the fowler, And from the perilous pestilence. He shall cover you will his feathers, and under his wings you shall take refuge; His truth shall be your sword and buckler." (Psalm 91:2-4 NKJV) Did you ever read that when days were dark and friends were few?

Come on Moses, tell us some more, and tell it good. Somebody needs to be reminded that you can guide us to patterns of survival in difficult times.

"You shall not be afraid of the terror by night, nor of the arrow that flies by day, Nor of the pestilence that walks in darkness, Nor for the destruction that lays waste at noonday. A thousand may fall at your side, and ten thousand at your right hand; But it shall not come near you." (Psalm 91:5-7 NKJV)

Oh, this is all in Psalm 91. I didn't write it, but I love to read it. I didn't say it. Moses said it over three thousand years ago. But it is still true now. Listen. "For he shall give his angels charge over you, to keep you in all your ways." (Psalm 91:11 NKJV)

Conclusion

The story is told of a family that was awakened by the piercing blare of their smoke detector to find that their house was on fire. The father ran into the kid's room and carried the 18 month old baby out in his arms, dragging the four year old by the hand.

They were halfway down the stairs when the little boy realized that he had left his teddy bear in his room. He broke away from his father to run and get it back. In the excitement and confusion, the father didn't notice that his son was not with him until he got outside. By now, the smoke was swirling around him. The boy cried out Daddy! Daddy ! Help Me!

His dad yelled from below, "Jump out of the window, Andy, I'll catch you"". "But I can't see you Daddy", the little boy cried. The father shouted back, "That's alright, I can see you. So jump."

So the boy jumped, and the father caught him in his arms and hugged him to his bosom.

When we are in our strait-jacket situations, with the flame and smoke swirling around us, as we stand in the window of disappointment, often we too, are unable to see God. The smoke of trials and tribulations, the fire of family feuds and fractured finances, the smoke of sickness and suffering, the fire of courts and trials; when the smoke cuts off our vision of our Father and we cry out "Father, I can't see you"; Our heavenly Father will always say, "that's alright, I can scc you. I will be there to catch you. Jump."

When you don't know where to turn, Jump.

When your best friends turn their backs on you, Jump.

When you've tried and failed in your trials, don't cry, don't try to figure out why, just Jump.

When I stand in the window, overlooking the valley of the shadow of death, My Father will tell me to Jump. Not into the oblivion of the grave, but into his everlasting, ever-loving arms.

He promised never to leave me alone . . . so I can just Jump.

He will wipe away all my tears . . . if I just Jump.

He will do the same for you . . . if you will only Jump.

And when I make my last Jump, God will—Oh I know he will—I have already asked him to . . .

Hide me in Thy Bosom

Oh, hide me in Thy bosom
Until the storm of life is o'er
And rock me in the cradle of Thy love
Oh, feed me Jesus, feed me; feed me Jesus feed me
Feed me Jesus, feed me; feed m,e Jesus feed me
Oh, until I want no more
And take me to Thy blessed home above.

(by Thomas A. Dorsey)

When You Are In A Strait-Jacket
Sermon 9: "Strike Me Down If I Am Lying"
By Rev. Dr. James D. Peters, Jr.

"Then let my arm fall from my shoulder, Let my arm be torn from the socket." (Job 31:22 NKJV)

Job was hurt. He thought he was dying. He felt forsaken, forgotten, abused and falsely accused. The one he held accountable was God. He was in a bind, in a strait-jacket.

One thing which people in this condition do is vacillate. The dictionary defines it as to sway to and fro: waver; totter; stagger; to fluctuate or oscillate; To waver in mind; show indecision.

While we marvel over the centuries at Job's patience, we would be blind to the facts if we did not notice his vacillating. From his strong pronouncement in Chapter 1, verse 21 when he said, "The Lord giveth and the Lord taketh away, blessed be the name of the Lord." Compare that to his prolific cursing in Chapter 3. Compare that to the moment when he dealt forthrightly with his grief, saying in 13:15 "Though he slay me, yet shall I trust in him." Compare that to the painful time when he said, "Man that is born of woman is few days and full of trouble:" (Job 14:1) Compare that to another high moment when he declared, "I know that my redeemer lives, and will stand at the latter day on the earth." (Job 19:25) It is easy to see that, in the midst of his terrible physical pain, he also had spiritual ups and downs.

If you have ever been in a strait-jacket kind of situation, or if you are in one now, passing through a kind of horrible, unpredictable situation, or if the time comes that you do, one thing is clear. You too have vacillated, or are vacillating, or will vacillate. You will move up and down the ladder of caring, of not caring; of loving or hating; of trusting God or wanting to challenge God. It is called vacillating. You know what I mean. You go back and forth. You know the meaning of being strong one moment and weak the next. In stout faith, Charles Albert Tindley wrote:

> *Trials dark on every hand, and we cannot understand*
> *All the ways that God would lead us to that blessed, promised*
> *land*
> *But He guides us with His eye and we'll follow till we die*
> *For we'll understand it better by and by.*

I have two points.

I. Job Wants His Day in Court

1.   Is this proper? What is the idea? Is he saying that God makes mistakes? Or that every time something bad happens, it means that God is punishing us? Job, like so many of us, tried to proclaim his innocence by saying: I am not guilty. Job, here, is calling a curse upon himself. He is saying to God, if I have sinned, let my shoulder fall away from my arm. If you say I am guilty, if you think I am lying, indict me. Have a preliminary hearing to see if there is probable cause. Try me. Impanel a jury of my peers. Let the prosecution present its case. Under cross examination, I will ask them to tell me the date, time and place when I did wrong.

It's as if he continues by saying: For my defense, I will be my own attorney. I will state my own case. I am not guilty. I don't deserve this. I love you, Lord. I trust you Lord. But you have not been fair to me. I thought you never made a mistake, Lord. But this time you've got the wrong man. Give me my day in court and my time to argue my case. If I am lying, strike me down. Let my arm fall from my shoulder blade. Let my arm be broken from the bone. Mess me up, Lord, if I have not told the truth.

2.   This is the last time Job speaks in these thirty-eight chapters with his vacillating comments, and included are the responses of his friends and Job's responses to his friends. But, here in Chapter 31 he proclaims, in vivid terms, his innocence of sins against the laws of God, and the omission of disobedience to the rules of human decency. He ends his many statements with the most solemn and elaborate protest of his innocence that he has ever tried to express. He states a number of specific areas in which he is not guilty. Let me point some of them out:

> *I did not treat my servants, male or female wrong in any way. (v. 13)*
> *I did not fail to help the poor or try in any way to hurt the widows. (v. 16)*
> *I did not forget the fatherless or the hungry. (v. 17)*
> *I did not keep clothing from the poor, If I had, they had. (v. 19)*
> *I was rich, but I did not worship my gold or my good things. (v. 24)*
> *I never gave worship to any creature which are due to God alone. (v. 26-28)*
> *If people did me wrong, I did not wish evil on them or curse them. (v. 29-30)*
> *I opened my door to strangers. (v. 32)*

So, make no mistake about it, Job was a good man. He stood in awe of the majesty of God and the wrath of God. He was saying, Lord, I was afraid to do wrong, yet I am being punished when I have been good. But with a clean past and a clear mind Job declares himself ready to face his judge, proud that his honor was still intact and his record unblemished. So against this background, Job makes his ultimate challenge to the God of creation.

Job cried out, "Oh that the Almighty would answer me; that my adversary would open a book filled with the charges against me and I declare I can answer every one." (v. 35) If I am lying, strike me down. Break my arm. Shatter my bones.

What we need to remember is that this whole story of Job is here to remind us that sin is not the cause of suffering. Yes, our own missteps and mistakes can bring us trouble. But God is not punishing us through sickness or sorrow for our sins. You don't need to remind God of how much good you have done when you find yourself in trouble. When trouble or disappointment comes into your life, don't spend time trying to find out what you did to cause it to happen. God is not waiting to find you weak and vulnerable to get even with you. God loves you. God will stand by you, even in your darkest hour. The ruler of the universe still rules. Your spirit may be locked in despair. Your movement may be restricted by circumstances beyond your control. But, God is the God of everybody, even when they are in trouble.

Trials dark on every hand, and we cannot understand,
All the ways that God would lead us to that blessed promised
land;
But He guides us with His eye and we'll follow till we die
We will understand it better by and by.

II.   The Danger of Talking Too Much

1.   Well, let's not be too hard on Job. For he was not the first or the last to want to ask questions of God. Even you have undoubtedly wanted to ask God why. When things happen which we don't understand, don't we want to ask God why? Why? Why did a certain person die? Oh yes, you have said: I have lived better than she has, why has this happened to me? I have been more faithful than he has been, why did this have to happen to me? In their hearts many human beings have wondered if God is aware of what's going on. They look at the injustices of life; the accidents which come out of unforeseen circumstances; the bitter blows of fate; the untimely visits from the angel of death, and ask God why? You stand near the bedside of a seriously ill loved one and ask God, Why? You see your life revised and rearranged and you ask God why? And you argue with God that something in the divine plan has gone wrong—that you don't deserve what's happening to you; that things should go better.

2.   One of the tragedies of life, even for those who seek spiritual direction, is that we often put our foot on the accelerator of a homemade theology, before we put the automatic transmission lever in 'DRIVE'. When you are facing things which you don't understand, you should remember to listen to God before speaking to and attempting to argue with Him. Job's trouble was that, in this case, he did not take time to think and meditate. When you are dealing with the 'divine whys', no real thought comes through except via silence and contemplation. You may want a roller coaster ride of challenging God. But when the thrill and frustration of your argument is over, you will still need to spend some quiet time in reflection and communication with God.

Some people talk too much. You may be one who talks too much. Who gave you divine insights about why things happen?

How can you possibly know why someone got sick; about why somebody didn't get a certain job; about why someone passed away; about why you are in a strait-jacket. You talk too much. About other people. About yourself. Quiet down. You don't know enough to attempt to challenge the veracity of God.

> *Temptations hidden snares*
> *Often take us unawares,*
> *And our hearts are made to bleed*
> *For many a thoughtless word or deed,*
> *And we wonder why the test*
> *When we try to do our best.*
> *But we'll understand it better by and by.*

Conclusion

1.   Job was angry. And anger hurts the person who is angry. It causes them to ask the wrong questions. It causes them to try to find someone to blame for their troubles. It causes them to sometimes argue with God. That is what the book of Job is all about: When your strait-jacket begins to pinch. When you feel that you have been in it too long. When you feel that you should not have been in it in the first place. What do you do? How do you challenge God?

Surely, what Job said here is not the answer. If I'm lying, strike me down. Is this kind of talk foreign to you? Have you ever heard anyone say anything similar? I have. Years ago, it was often that you heard someone proposing this strange bargain. If I'm lying, let the Lord strike me stone dead. If I'm lying, let lightning strike me now. Some people used to say things just like that.

Job is again arguing his case. He is telling God that a divine mistake has been made. That he, Job, has been a very good man and that he does not deserve what has happened to him.

For proof of his claim he offers this preposterous proposition. His words ring across the years. Lord, if I lie, if I did not help the poor, the prison bound, the poor in spirit, then you deal with me. Strike me down if I am lying.

In the same vein, though in different circumstances, we find the Psalmist mourning the problems of the Children of Israel being captives in Babylon. In Psalm 137:5-6 we find these words. "If I forget thee, O Jerusalem, let my right hand forget her cunning. If I do not remember thee, let my tongue cleave to the roof of my mouth." In other words the writer said, Lord, if I forget You, let my right hand forget how to write and my tongue forget how to talk.

Keep quiet when you are telling God, 'Strike me down if I am lying'. Keep quiet when you feel like asking God for a reason for things you don't understand. When you hurt the most, God knows and God will be there for you. You don't need to go the court of divine justice to prove your goodness. Just keep quiet and wait on the Lord. You see, your intelligence is too flawed, too limited to argue with God. Your debating ability is too limited whether you are doing direct examination, cross examination, redirect or re-cross. Your theology is too shallow. In the words of that Broadway musical based on a book written by Vinnette Carroll "Your Arms Are Too Short To Box With God" So, Cool it! Back Off! Calm Down.

Instead of saying 'Strike me down if I am lying', try singing these lyrics from a familiar hymn written in 1907:

Have thine own way, Lord!
Have thine own way!
Thou art the potter,
I am the clay
Mold me and make me
After thy will

While I am waiting
Yielded and still.

Instead of saying 'Strike me down if I am lying', use these words from another song entitled "Someday" by Tindley, and say:

Burdens now may press me down
Dis-appointments all around
Troubles speak with mournful sigh
Sorrow through a tear-stained-eye

There is a world where pleasure reigns
No mourning soul shall roam it's plains
And to that land of peace and glory
I want to go someday

I do not know how long it will be
Nor what the future holds for me
But, this I know if Jesus leads me
I shall get home someday.

Instead of saying 'Strike me down if I am lying', change your tune by saying:

By and by when the morning comes,
When all the saints of God are gathered home,
We'll tell the story of how we have overcome
For we'll understand it better by and by.

WHEN YOU ARE IN A STRAIT-JACKET
Sermon 10: "Can You Sing Songs In The Night?"
By Rev. Dr. James D. Peters, Jr.

"But no one says, 'Where is God my Maker, Who gives songs in the night, Who teaches us more than the beasts of the earth, and makes us wiser than the birds of heaven?'" (Job 35.10-11 NKJV)

Here we have an appeal being made to Job to have faith in God, and to trust God's justice and depend on God to bring him out of trouble. I know it may seem shocking for some to hear of a man whose name is not well known, telling a seasoned spiritual soldier like Job, to hold on and trust and be patient. But, God gives us truth, sometimes out of the mouths of babes and sucklings. For no matter who we are, as the song goes "Everybody needs somebody sometimes." And on this night of sadness for Job, he needed someone like Elihu to remind him that God was his maker, and that God gives songs in the night.

So the words of Elihu ring across the centuries to challenge us today. Too often, he says, people in trouble focus on their problems and fears instead of saying, "Where is God my maker who gives songs in the night? His word, and God's message to you who may be in trouble today is that instead of looking to the right or left, to find an escape from your trouble, that you look to the hills from whence comes your help. For, your real help comes from the Lord who made heaven and earth.

It is night when: You think that God has forgotten you; or you feel that God does not care what happens to you; or you think that God is punishing you unjustly.

I ask you this challenging question. When you are in a strait-jacket, "Can you sing songs in the night?" I have two points.

I. Anyone Can Sing in Good Times

1.   Who is it that must sing songs in the night? Well, it is the person going through a strait-jacket kind of experience. It is the person who, like Job, is in real trouble. Anybody can sing in the daytime. Anybody can sing when all is well in their circumstances; or when their cup is running over; or when they are living under the abundance of life's plenty. Anybody can sing when your home is reasonably happy, when your job is secure, when your health is stable.

It's easy to sing when you can read the notes by daylight, by candlelight, by electric light. But it is the spiritually skillful singer who can sing when there is not a ray of light to read by. It is the stout-hearted soul who can sing from their heart, despite having no light by which to read or way of reading. When your songs must come from that living book which dwells in the depths of your soul, that is night singing.

I think that anybody could sing a song of joy after God has opened the waters of the Red Sea for the children of Israel and drowned the Egyptians in the rushing waters. Do you remember the song of Moses?

I will sing to the Lord, for He has triumphed gloriously!
The horse and his rider has He thrown into the sea!

The challenge would have been to compose a song of faith before the Red Sea had been divided and to sing it before Pharaoh's host had been drowned. You see, it's hard to sing when doubt and darkness and fear live in your heart. Songs of faith in the night seasons of life, in the strait-jacket times in your life, come only from God. In the dark night of trouble, God's song may be your only song.

2.   For, no matter who you are, life has its night seasons. The sun shines by day. But toward evening the darkness seems to pull the cord on the window drapes, and the evening shadows fall. In the course of things, the fact that night comes is a great blessing. Yet, the night seasons of life are, for many, a gloomy time. There is the "Pestilence that walks in darkness." Yes, even the night has its glorious songs.

Have you ever stood by the seaside at night and heard the song of the water as it cascades over the stones? Have you ever stood on the quiet of a beach at night and watched the waves ripple, seemingly singing a merry song beneath the stars? Did you ever imagine that you could hear the harp of God, playing a song of faith on the chords of your soul? Night has its songs. We don't need very much poetry in our spirits to catch the songs of night. A heavenly choir seems to chant anthems of praise to God which are loud in the heart, even if they are silent in the ear.

3.   Songs in the night do not arise spontaneously. There is something paradoxical, almost contradictory in the phrase, "songs in the night." For when we think of songs, we tend to think of good times. Yet, this reference to songs in the night refers to the troubled times of life. The night songs to which Elihu refers are a contradiction in light of the pain which Job

is feeling. He is talking about pure and refreshing gladness, as is indicated by his reference to "God my Maker", as the source of power. Elihu's night songs are of holy thought and heavenly music. Now, sorrow does not produce the songs of night. If we are to enjoy deep harmonies of thought, or to soar unto high heavens of emotion among the depressing influences of trouble, we must not look for the trouble to produce the songs. We must turn elsewhere. If all of our focus is on the here and now, the physical and that which we can hold in our hands, then we can hardly find inner peace in troubled times. The kind of songs which Elihu spoke of will usually not be ours to sing.

Songs in the night are given by God. In the still hours of darkness and pain and problems, God draws near to the soul. When the desolation and misery are greatest, God is most compassionate. You see, God is not dependent on external circumstances. Night and day are alike to him. True, it is possible for him to inspire his sweetest songs when we are drinking from the most bitter cup. But we must not delude ourselves into the notion that we shall not feel suffering if God is with us. Even when He gives us a song, the song does not dispel the darkness of night. But it can drive out the terror and the despair, and bring peace and the deep joy which you need to make it over the strait-jacket times. A secular song with a strong ring of faith, entitled "Stand By Me" says:

When the night has come, And the land is dark
And the moon is the only light we'll see
No I won't be afraid. Oh I won't be afraid.
Just as long as you stand by me.

If the sky that we look upon
Should tumble and fall
Or the Mountain should crumble to the sea
I won't, I won't cry, No I won't shed a tear
Just as long as you stand by me.

II. Memories Play a Part in Singing Night Songs

1.   Have you forgotten that your mind is a storehouse of memories? Your soul is a reservoir of special memories. In the rural areas where people use wells, some kinds of wells had a pump on them. When you wanted some water you first had to prime the pump. You had to pour some water in, before you could get some water out. You had to have a little before you could get a lot.

When you need something to prime your spiritual pump, go to God. Take it to the Lord in prayer. For God is the composer of songs and the teacher of music. God is the one who can turn back the pages of your memory and remind you of the dangers seen and unseen through which God has brought you. God is the one who can do the same thing for you now. God can teach you to sing songs in the night. One song writer said it like this.

> *Precious memories, unseen angels,*
> *Sent from somewhere to my soul*
> *How they linger, ever near me,*
> *And the sacred past unfolds*
>
> *Precious memories, how they linger,*
> *How they ever flood my soul*
> *In the stillness of the midnight,*
> *Precious, sacred scenes unfold.*

2.   Do you have some memories that time cannot erase? Go back into your personal archives. I don't know about you, but whenever I am tempted to be sad, I just focus on the good old days. [They might be recent or years back.] But the good old days were days when I know that God was talking with me and walking with me, and reminding me not to worry. We tend to forget too soon, how much the Lord had done for

us in the past. When the pinch of our personal strait-jacket, and the length of time we have had to wear it, have us feeling downtrodden, when we feel we are about to come apart at the seams, we need to take a stroll down memory lane. If God has ever done anything very special for you, gotten you out of trouble which seemed that it would crush you, delivered you when you thought deliverance was impossible, how can you forget? Think about it right now, and I declare that it will help you right now. One song writer said it like this:

How I got over, How I got over,
Lord, my soul looked back and wondered
How I got over.
How I got over, How I got over
My soul looked back and wondered How I got over.

Lord, I've been 'buked and I've been scorned
And I've been talked about as sure as you're born.
And my soul looked back and wondered, how I got over.

3.   Songs in the night may be enjoyed. Elihu speaks in the present tense, which means right then. The biblical record tells of many a soul cheered by heavenly songs in darkest hours. Paul and Silas had no logical reason to be singing in the Philippian jail. It had been a rough day. They had been treated unfairly and unfriendly. They had been falsely accused and publicly beaten. They had been thrown in jail on trumped up charges. And with pain in their bodies, and troubled in their spirits, a peculiar sound came out of the Philippian jail at midnight. There was singing and praying going on. These itinerant preachers, these traveling sky pilots, these absurd apostles were singing in the jail at midnight. Yes, there can be no doubt, they were singing songs in the night.

Sometimes it takes the midnight hour in our lives to make us know that what we need is . . . .

Rev. Dr. James D. Peters, Jr.

Not a minor tuneup, but a major overhaul.
Not a shift in focus, but a total change of direction
Not a transfusion, but a heart transplant.

And, just like God delivered Paul and Silas through their midnight prayer meeting, you can be delivered also.

You can do it too. Do you know that? Have you ever done it? Do you want to learn how to do it again? Those who trust in God have been given inner joy, even when their outer life has been hard and cruel. The joy of God is never so real as when it breaks out in the midst of the deepest earthly trouble. This is an actual escape from the feeling of despair, even when you feel that you have gone to your extreme.

Conclusion

How do I know that we can sing songs in the night seasons of our lives? There are two reasons.

1.   Scripture sings to me through God's majestic power in nature. God spreads out a star-studded canopy in the skies which caused David to sing this beautiful song:

"When I consider Your heavens, the work of Your fingers, The moon and the stars, which You have ordained, What is man that You are mindful of him, And the son of man that You visit him? For You have made him a little lower than the angels, And You have crowned him with glory and honor." (Psalm 8:3-5)

In spite of his own personal difficulties, it was David who sang this:

"Oh come, let us sing to the Lord! Let us shout joyfully to the Rock of our salvation. Let us come before His presence with thanksgiving; Let us shout joyfully to Him with psalms. For the Lord is a great God, And the King above all gods. In His hand are the deep places of the earth: The heights of the hills are His also." (Psalm 95:1-4 NKJV)

A momentary vision of the majesty of God causes Isaiah to sing:

"Lift up your eyes on high, and see who has created these things, Who brings out their host by number: He calls them all by name, By the greatness of His might And the strength of His power, not one is missing." (Isaiah 40:26 NKJV)

And was it not a noble song which Paul sent forth to his young son Timothy in his death bed song from Nero's prison?

"For I am now ready to be offered, and the time of my departure is at hand. I have fought a good fight, I have finished my course, I have kept the faith:" (II Timothy 4:6-7 KJV)

The second reason I know that we can sing songs in the night is because I have done it so many times myself. Many times have come when I had to face my own strait-jacket situations. There were times when I, too, couldn't seem to get a prayer through. But I have found that when God gave me a song, deliverance surely did come. It is like this, as sung by Bobby Jones:

God gave me a song that the angels cannot sing.
I've been washed in the blood, of the crucified one.
I've been redeemed.

The Lord has been so good to me.
He opened doors I could not see
Sometimes when I am feeling low
No one to hear, no place to go

God gave me a song.

When You Are In A Strait-Jacket
Sermon 11: "Can You Speak on God's Behalf?"
By Rev. Dr. James D. Peters, Jr.

"Elihu also proceeded, and said: Bear with me a little, and I will show you that there are yet words to speak on God's behalf." (Job 36.1-2 NKJV)

God is wonderful, Glorious, Almighty, and all powerful. Why should God need you or me or any human being to speak on His behalf? He speaks through an earthquake and through a storm-tossed sea. He speaks through a silent night so sweet and quietly. Why should God need someone to speak on His behalf? I'll tell you why.

It is because we speak the language, we feel the pain, and we feel the abandonment which other humans feel. Most of us have been there—in life's Emergency Rooms, in life's Intensive Care Unit rooms, in the Courtrooms, in the Hearing Rooms, in the Morticians Offices, in funeral services and in graveyard settings. Because we have had our own strait-jacket experiences, we can best speak on God's behalf when some other child of the flesh is feeling forsaken. I need to hear it from you. You need to hear it from me. When my dreams have been compromised, when your hopes have been postponed, when your life has been rearranged, when we are tempted, like Job, to blame God for what has happened to us. Somebody needs to speak on God's behalf.

You don't have to do it. Yes, God can speak for God. God can handle heaven's own affairs. You will see God speaking very soon now in this book of Job. If you fail to speak, somehow it will be done. But the question is, can you do it? Can you speak on God's behalf?

Remember, this was not Job talking. These are the words of the young man who had listened to all that he could endure and felt that he had to say something. His name was Elihu. This is part of the story of the problems, troubles, patience and sometimes the impatience of Job. This is a real question. This is a good question. When everything seems to be going against you; when it is like you are in a hopeless situation, can you speak on Gods' behalf?

These two chapters of 36 and 37 form a single speech by Elihu. They constitute the last appeal to Job, who is being asked, even begged, to accept the fact of God's inscrutability or God's ultimate fairness. He seeks to prove his right to offer counsel to Job, by declaring that he has not yet spoken on God's behalf. What he is really saying is that, somebody ought to speak for the fairness and goodness of God, even in strait-jacket kinds of situations. I ask, can you do it? I have two points.

I. Needed—Someone to Speak for God

1. Elihu stands like an unpopular preacher declaring nevertheless that someone has to speak up. God will not commission an ambassador without giving them a message. It is a great privilege and a great responsibility to speak to human beings on God's behalf. To tell people in troubled times that God still loves them. To proclaim that, in spite of terrible tragedies both personal and public, that God still has power. Even in bad times, it must be said. To say anything else is to profane the sacred. The fact that we don't understand

everything which happens to us does not mean, as Job felt in his weak moments, that God does not care.

2.   In tough times, when you seem to be in a strait-jacket, don't be tempted to make rash statements, or form unwarranted deductions about God. You don't form your theology, and you don't develop your concepts of God when you are passing through a Hothouse of Tears. You don't cry out about the unfairness of God when you are hurting from sores from the top of your head to the soles of your feet, like Job. In those times just remember that, "those who wait on the Lord shall renew their strength." (Isaiah 40:31 NKJV)

Job and his three friends are good examples of people who look at the same circumstance from different points of view, and all declare that the others are wrong. Elihu tries to look at divine truth as a many-sided thing, with deep personal reflection. He allows himself to be immersed in careful introspection, inspection and meditation. His word is this. While so many bad things are happening to you, you need to know that now is not forever. Somebody needs to speak out for God, to say a word on God's behalf.

3.   Elihu begins verse 5 of this dissertation with the word, "Behold". To get Job's attention and our attention he says, 'behold' or 'look here'. It reads, "Behold, God is mighty, but despises no one; He is mighty in strength of understanding." He is telling Job that he insinuated that God turned a deaf ear to his pain and his misery. But he is also telling Job, and many of us who are known to have limited patience and a short fuse in difficult times, that God still cares. That the Supreme Governor of the Universe is too exalted a Being to act unjustly, or even unkindly, toward any of his creatures. When God, on Creation Morning made everything, God's own commentary was that it was 'Good'. God does not despise that which He made. God made you and God loves you. The roads may get rough and the

circumstances may be unpredictable, and you may not know just what's going to happen next. But God is still God.

God, with the combination of strength and beauty, of power and gentleness, of dignity and condescension, of standing high and looking low, is first and last a God of love and caring. The Divine Being can penetrate through all disguises, discovering right and wrong everywhere, at all times, and in all circumstances.

Now, we must admit that Elihu seems a bit bold to declare that he is speaking on God's behalf. It takes nerve to do this. He may be right, but his claim needs to be tested. You can't just take the word of anyone who claims to speak for God. Not all who come in prophet's clothing are accredited as God's Ambassadors. We must examine the credentials of those who say they speak for God. We must try the Spirit by the Spirit. We must test the truth of the words of those who claim to speak for God by the proven words of those who have already spoken for God. Don't take my word at face value unless it is in accord with what Isaiah and Jeremiah and Paul and Peter said.

There are times when God requires people to speak for Him, and we dare not be silent. Wrong must be denounced; error must be corrected; truth must be maintained; the good news of the Gospel must be made known. It is only by having a Divine Commission that I am allowed to speak for God. Those who speak for God must be called by God. This you must know when you try to give advice to someone who has lost a loved one, or who is wrestling with some of the "Why Me Lord" kinds of questions. Be sure that, before you try to talk to them, that you know, as the songwriter said:

That God is a good God.
He's a great God
He can do anything but fail

> *He has moved so many mountains out of my way*
> *God is a wonderful God.*

When you know that, then you can tell somebody what God is like.

II.   God Still Loves and Cares For You

1.   God does not withdraw his eyes from His children, whether kings or prisoners. This is repeated over and over in II Chronicles 16:9; where we find: "For the eyes of the Lord run to and fro throughout the whole earth, to show himself strong in the behalf of them whose heart is perfect toward him."

In Psalm 46:1-2 we find "God is our refuge and strength, a very present help in trouble. Therefore will not we fear, though the earth be removed and though the mountains be carried into the midst of the sea."

In Psalm 91:1-2 we find "He who dwells in the secret place of the most High shall abide under the shadow of the Almighty. I will say of the Lord, He is my refuge and my fortress; My God; in him will I trust."

God's love and care worked for kings like David, Solomon, Hezekiah and Josiah. It worked for prisoners in affliction like Joseph in Egypt, or Daniel in Babylon or Paul in the Phillipian jail. In every instance, God shows his loving care primarily by and through His word and His Holy Spirit.

Elihu said, Job you, in spite of being a holy, good man, a God fearing man, you, like the wicked, have pronounced a judicial sentence upon God and His dealings with you. You have accused God of being unfair to you. No wealth or education or status or even being close to God can save you from some of the burdens of life. Nothing will, for life is unpredictable.

2.   This present word from the lips of Elihu, shows us that he rises to a sublime view of God as the infinitely Mighty One, the wise and just Father of the human family. As we have seen so often in reading the Bible, this is the firm foundation—truth, the basic first truth, which runs beneath the whole of this book of Job.

Suffering and pain come at some time to everyone of us. Then comes the visitation of God to open our ears to hear and our eyes to see the salvation of God. The season of depression and disaster will pass, and the sheep who have heard the voice of the Shepherd will find themselves led once more into green pastures. For, no matter how tight the strait-jacket, the believers can still say, "the Lord is still my shepherd, I shall not want." (Psalm 23:1)

The teacher must be taught. The advocate must have their own belief. The Envoy must know where he came from. The Ambassador must be appointed by the Head of State. When someone's life is falling apart, you can't help them unless you know what God has done and what God is able to do.

3.   When you travel by faith, you must be able to look at the big picture. If you measure your trust in God by how you feel when "Days are dark and friends are few", be sure to look at the big picture.

Tell me, when you look back after five or ten years, did God ever forsake you? When you look at forty or fifty years, did God ever let you down? No.

In a song recorded by various artists, the writer told you, and I just reminded you that:

God is a good God,
He's a great God.

He can do anything but fail.
Did God ever move any mountains out of your way?
He has for me.
He will for you.
I know he can, I know he will
He'll fight your battles if you just keep still.

Conclusion

Job's final speech, which began at Chapter 26 and ends with Chapter 31 is firstly an answer to the words of Bildad, the Shuhite, in chapter 25. But primarily Job's words are a complaint against God whom he feels has been unfair to him. For, while Job is known for his patience—he could not understand why he suffered so much when he had done nothing wrong.

Job dressed his remarks in brilliant poetry, and disguises his pain in dramatic rhetoric. In Chapter 27, verses 1-5 moreover Job continued his discourse, and said, "As God lives, who has taken away my justice, And the almighty, who has made my soul bitter, As long as breath is in me, and the breath of my God is in my nostrils, my lips will not speak, nor my tongue utter deceit. Be it far from me that I should say you are right; till I die I will not put away my integrity from me."

His words are deep. His way of saying them is indeed poetic. But still he is crying out of his pain. And he is confused, and yes, he is angry with God.

So Elihu says in our text (Job 36:2): Give me some time. Don't cut me off now. Wait a little while and keep listening to me. Let me finish my words, for I have not yet spoken on God's behalf. I will gather my knowledge from afar, and will ascribe righteousness to my maker.

The Hebrew word used here for God is just "El". Not El Shadda, or Elohim, just El. When you are on speaking terms with God, you don't have to use a lot of formality, just say, God.

So, speak on behalf of God, as I have done this for a long time. I will continue as long as I can. But, do you know what is going to happen to me? One day I won't be able to speak for God. I may not even be able to speak for myself. I will stand before the bar of eternal justice. And I will not measure up to the demands of divine justice. In spite of my good intentions, I will have fallen short of the glory of God. I will say to the Judge of Righteousness, I tried. But my best will still be just filthy rags in the holy light of Divine Presence; When I stand stripped before the bar, my years of service will not help me; My degrees will make no difference; My spotted history will not get me over. I will need someone to speak on my behalf. All I will be able to do for myself is plead the blood of Jesus.

And, do you know what? If I have spoken on God's behalf to people about to give up, God will speak for me in the hour when I need it most. God will own me and claim me as His child.

Where will I stand on that day when I can't stand for myself? How will I stand? On what basis can I stand?

Standing on the Promises of Christ my King
Through eternal ages let His praises Ring
Glory in the highest, I will shout and sing
Standing on the promises of God.

Standing on the promises that cannot fail.
When the howling storms of doubt and fear assail
By the living word of God I shall prevail
Standing on the promises of God.

(Published in 1886 by Russell K. Carter)

When You Are In a Strait-Jacket
Sermon 12: "Can You Comprehend God?"
By Rev. Dr. James D. Peters, Jr.

"God thunders marvelously with his voice; He does great things which we cannot comprehend." (Job 37:5 NKJV)

Comprehend. Definition: To catch hold of, to seize, to grasp mentally, to understand, to take in. Some would say that we humans can never, ever even begin to comprehend God. But, let us explore and see if we do comprehend God in some ways or seasons of our lives.

We see the forces of nature. You see, but you do not fully understand. Like Jesus said to Nicodemus, "The wind blows where it wishes, and you hear the sound of it, but cannot tell where it comes from and where it goes. Where the wind blows you do not know." (John 3:8a NKJV)

In the midst of Elihu's words to Job, he is suddenly startled into a mixture of terror and admiration at the awesome power of God as shown in a thunderstorm. In his description of the thunderstorm, Elihu dwells on its marvelous power. Each step in the process of the storm is strange and wonderful, beyond a human being's comprehension. What he is trying to point out is that other kinds of storms come which are also, truly wonderful.

Storms can come quickly in life. He uses the occurrence of this sudden storm to talk about the power of God—the booming thunder, the flashing lightning, the boisterous wind.

He realizes that God is in complete control of all of these natural events which are around all of them. Likewise, when storms come into your life, even in strait-jacket times, they come not to destroy you, but to prepare you.

Yet, Elihu is saying to Job and to all of us, that while we can accept the power of God in nature, we have a problem understanding, comprehending God, in our own times of trouble. Life is like that: sunshine and shadows, good days and bad days, harmony and discord, mountains and valleys. Life is like that. When you are in a strait jacket, can you comprehend God? I have two points.

I.   Comprehending God in Good Times

1.   We do rather well comprehending, and understanding God, in good times. When good things happen, most of the time we will give God the credit for His blessings to us.

This is not to say that we don't slip sometimes. Remember that Old Testament great warning from God found in Deuteronomy 6:10-12? "So it shall be, when the Lord your God brings you into the land of which He swore to your fathers, to Abraham, Isaac, and Jacob, to give you large and beautiful cities, which you did not build, 'houses full of all good things, which you did not fill, hewn-out wells which you did not dig, vineyards and olive trees, which you did not plant—when you have eaten and are full . . . . then beware, lest you forget the Lord who brought out of the land of Egypt, from the house of bondage."

Even this suggests that our first inclination is to give credit to God, even if after a while, we are tempted to forget God.

As Mahalia Jackson sang it:

> *God is so good to me,*
> *God is so good to me*
> *I don't serve him as I should,*
> *I don't deserve all of this good*
> *So many things are not as they should be*
> *But, God is so good to me.*

2. Some people have trouble, after a while, with comprehending God in good times. The great temptation is to think that you did it all by yourself, that you were just smart, that you came from good stock, that you picked yourself up by your own boot straps, that you beat the odds all by yourself.

But most people, especially if they believe and trust in God, can give God the credit. They can be a witness to the overall goodness and love of God. That's where Job started. Before this great test of his patience, even God said that Job was a good man, one who feared God, who respected God, and who appreciated God, in good times.

3. A secular song writer, in his romantic musings said these words long ago:

> *The greatest thing in all this world*
> *Is just to love and be loved in return.*

I suggest that this is true emotionally, mentally, and physically. There is probably nothing more lovely than to see two people standing before an altar, pledging their mutual love and caring to each other—

> *To have and to hold from this day forward.*
> *For better or worse,*
> *For richer or for poorer;*

In sickness or in health;
To love and to cherish;
Till death do us part.

But, probably there is nothing sadder when, or if, the warm milk of love turns into the sour cream of hate. When people who have been so close that they could feel each other's pain become instead, a source of pain which is reflected in physical or emotional battering and blaming, in fussing and cussing.

Likewise, spiritually, there is nothing more precious than a human being acknowledging and appreciating God. One who could say, or sing, from the depths of their heart, these words written by Charles Nicks:

I really love the Lord,
I really love the Lord
You don't know what he's done for me
He gave me the victory
I love Him, I love Him,
I really love the Lord.

But there is nothing more pitiful than to see a person who used to love the Lord, who used to walk with the Lord, who used to go to church, who used to love going to church, who used to love serving God and working in the church, singing, ushering teaching, praying, giving their time, giving their money—

To see this person who grew up in the church; who knew the beauty of a faith full of sincere belief that God could and would save, heal, guide and deliver.

To see such a person come to the Red Sea place in their lives; to see them, sometimes through no fault of their own, placed in an emotional strait-jacket: one so tight that the more they struggle against it, the more it hurts; to see them unable to comprehend God.

To see them turn away from God. Stop coming to church. Or even worse, for them to keep coming to church, but not really be there. To see them in the worship, but not really be in the service. To see them in the house where sacred fires are burning, but they are not feeling the heat of the spiritual flames.

There are some people today who are in that condition; that kind of personal pain. Even in good times, life can create distance from God when the picture is blurred in their vision.

II. Comprehending God in Bad Times

1. In difficult times, in strait-jacket times, often our ability to comprehend God, even our vision of God is way out of focus. In times of grief, depression, pain and problems, we seem to have a hard time putting a loving God in perspective. We, like Job are often ready to turn on God when we are hurting. We sometimes tend to be messed up, mixed up, in discord, in disarray.

When the strait-jacket is used, and when it seems to be put on us personally; through our family; our employment; our circle of close friends; our health; our financial resources—we sometimes seem to lose it; to argue with God, to get angry with God.

2. When did Job change? It was when bad things suddenly happened to Job. It was when his whole life was turned upside down; when his noonday turned to midnight; when suddenly, everything he had was gone.

It was a time when it seemed that there was no one who cared about him; that there was no one for him to really talk to; no one to laugh with; nothing to laugh about. When under the pressure of his personal strait-jacket, he felt that God had forgotten him or, even worse, turned against him.

This man Job, who felt that he had a clear picture, a close connection, a good understanding, a real comprehension of God, suddenly he felt cheated, betrayed, and attacked on his blind side. He felt that if God did not do these things to him, God surely permitted these terrible to happen to him. And he knew that he did not deserve it. And that life and God were being unfair to him.

3.   When this happens to us we tend to become confused. We felt that God loved us, but we wondered why we found ourselves in a strait-jacket. Here we are: Unable to move emotionally, unable to function normally, unable to think straight, unable to sing the Lord's song in this strange condition. Sometimes we feel that we are even unable to get a prayer through.

In many ways, in painful circumstances like these, we cannot even begin to comprehend God. At least we feel that we cannot understand God at a time like this. Not during this period of our lives. Perhaps when we get to glory, we'll comprehend it, but not now.

This must have been what Fanny J. Crosby meant when she wrote the words of this hymn:

> *There are depths of love that I cannot know*
> *Till I cross the narrow sea*
> *There are heights of joy that I can not reach*
> *Till l rest in peace with thee.*

Conclusion

So, what is the answer to the question proposed here? Can you comprehend God? And if some people have trouble understanding God in times of terrible trouble, what happens to our faith in God at that time? I want to tell you, if you don't know, or to remind you in case you have forgotten, that God loves you. That the same God you once knew is still in charge of the destiny of human beings. Faith in God may not change your circumstances, but it will change the way you respond to the circumstances which occur in your life.

So, what is the answer? Can you, can I, comprehend God? No! The human mind cannot ever fully comprehend God. It becomes extremely difficult in uncertain times. But you can comprehend enough of what God is and what God is all about, to survive. I am not an electrician. I know absolutely nothing about connecting positive and negative wires. But, I don't need that kind of knowledge to just flip the light switch and turn the light on. I know enough to get light.

Using my inspired imagination, I dramatize this incident this way:

Moses, in a very difficult time, said these words to God. "Lord the people think that I am the closest one to You. But, Lord, I don't fully understand you either. So, don't just talk to me, come down to my tent and talk to me face to face. This way I can understand you, I can comprehend You, more fully. God said, No! Moses you could not stand it. No human being can see my face and live. You just come out to where the cave ends and you can get a view of the mountainside. I will just pass by. Moses did what God said and God did what He promised. God passed by and Moses saw the flowing of the robes of God. And—that was enough, to remind Moses that it was God who got water out of the rock and bread from the sky. Enough, to make Moses know that it was God, who gave him strength in his old age. Enough, to take him from the wilderness to the top of Mt. Pisgah. Enough, to last him for the rest of his life.

Here it is from the book of Exodus: "But He said, 'You cannot see my face; for no man can see me and live.' And the Lord said 'Here is a place by Me, and you shall stand on the rock. So it shall be, while My glory passes by, that I will put you in the cleft of the rock, and will cover you with My hand while I pass by. Then I will take away My hand, and you shall see My back, but My face shall not be seen." (Exodus 33:20-23 NKJV)

So, I just believe that even in strait-jacket times, you can see, you can understand enough of God to last you until you reach the place where God will make it clear.

The story is told of a college student who returned to his room with his friend and roommate. He opened his emails, read one, bowed his head for a moment, shook his head, opened the dresser, got his suitcase and began to pack his things. His roommate asked what was wrong. He copied the email and handed a copy to his roommate. It said, "Something has happened, check out of school and come home right away." The roommate asked what was wrong and the answer was "I don't know". The roommate said you can't just go home just like that. Your education is important to you. Why don't you ask him why? The son said, "The email is real. It is from my father. He is my father and when I get there, he will tell me why!"

So, my weary and wondering, questioning friends, regarding the mysteries of life which you cannot possibly understand, when you get home, your Heavenly Father will tell you why.

The Apostle Paul said: "For now we see in a mirror dimly, but then face to face. Now I know in part, but then I shall know just as I also am known." (I Corinthians 13:12 NKJV)

Farther along we'll know all about it.
Farther along we'll understand why;
Cheer up my brother, live in the sunlight
We'll understand it all by and by.

(Attributed to W. B. Stevens, 1911)

WHEN YOU ARE IN A STRAIT-JACKET
Sermon 13: "How Do You Fathom the Questions of God?" Pt 1 of 3
Rev. Dr. James D. Peters, Jr.

"Where were you when I laid the foundations of the earth? Tell me, if you have understanding. Who determined its measurements? Surely you know! Or who stretched the line upon it?" (Job 38:4-5 NKJV)

"How do you fathom the questions of God?" There are many definitions found in the dictionary for fathom and most of them deal with depths of water. But the one which commands our interest today is the one which defines fathom as, "To get to the bottom of, to understand thoroughly." We all want answers from God. We want to know why things happen as they do. We seem to want to know from God—the who, what, when, why, and how of life. In many ways we are just like Job.

Job's cries have been pathetic. His wail is one which most of us can understand. His faith has been up and down, back and forth, like the faith of many of us. At one point he was saying, even through his tears, "Though He slay me, yet will I trust in him." (Job 13:15a NKJV) Yet, at other times his cry is that God has been unfair and he is asking, begging for a chance to confront God, to debate with God, to argue with God.

In Chapter 37, we looked at the questions which Elihu asked of Job. But here in Chapter 38, the whole picture changes. It is now God who asks the questions. Responding to all of the many words of Job, found in various places from Chapter 3 to Chapter 31, in particular to words like those uttered in 23:3 where Job cried out "Oh that I knew where I might find Him! that I might come to his seat! I would present my case before him, and fill my mouth with arguments." Now God speaks, saying, come on Job, let me ask some questions, and you try to answer me.

Dr. Derring E. King, the late preacher from Chicago gave a dramatic twist to God's questioning moment. What he said was that "God rolled up in a late model whirlwind. He did not get out of the whirlwind, but spoke from with the whirlwind."

This is some of the most classic of biblical poetry. These questions from God to Job must be viewed as questions to all of us, especially in our times of trouble. These many questions cover so much of life itself and are so numerous that, for the purposes of these series of sermons, I have broken down these questions from God into three general areas. First, God asking, What do you know about nature? 2nd, What do you know about evil in the world? and 3rd, What do you know about death? These will be the specific focus of this and the next two sermons.

You know how it starts. In Job 38:1 "Then the Lord answered Job out of the whirlwind, and said. Who is this that darkens counsel without knowledge?" When Job felt more alone than he had ever felt in his life. When all of the human words had been spoken, God spoke. The implication of this is most clear. When the most pressing crisis comes, yes even when we are in our physical, social or emotional strait-jackets, God will speak.

For when you question God, sooner or later the roles are reversed and the really important questions are raised. The ultimate dilemma of human existence lies not in God's failure to answer human beings, but in our inability to answer God.

Well did Matthew Henry say "In most disputes the question is who will have the last word. Job's friends had, in this controversy, tamely yielded it to Job, and then to Elihu. But, after all the wrangling of the prosecution and defense counsel at the bar, the judge upon the bench must have the last word; so God had here, and so God will have in every controversy, for every person's judgment proceeds from God and by God's definitive sentence every person's case must stand or fall and every cause be won or lost. Job had often appealed to God and had talked boldly about how he, as a prince, would go near to God. But, when God took the throne, Job has nothing to say in his own defense. It is not an easy matter, as some think, to enter a contest with the Almighty."

What God said was "gird up your loins like a man. I will question you and you will answer me." So, God asks Job and I ask you, How Do you Fathom the Questions of God? Let's just combine the questions about nature in this sermon. I have two points.

I.   What Do You Know About Light and Darkness?

1.   You can see that I have picked some of the easy ones, for God's first question was "Where were you when I laid the foundations of the earth." So, dealing with something seemingly simple like light and darkness should give us a good start on the questions of God. We all know, or think we know something about the dawn. Why, we have had the chance to see it almost all of the days of our lives. In the language of many poets we are told that "Dawn lifts up the darkness as the veil under which the earth has been asleep and shakes the night

out of the blanket of darkness which has covered the night." The descriptions are vivid. It is dawn when the earth awakens, the sunrise sharply accentuates and reddens its configurations. Dawn—when the night puts on a new dress, and is decked out in brilliance. Dawn—as described by Paul Lawrence Dunbar in his beautiful poem by that name, with these words of great poetry and meaning.

> *"An angel robed in spotless white*
> *bent down to kiss the sleeping night*
> *night woke to blush, the spite was gone*
> *men saw the blush and called it dawn.*

2.   It is so simple, so ordinary, a part of every morning. But how do you explain it? How do you, a mere human being, explain to God how you fathom something as simple as the rapid changes from day to night, and night to day, and day to night again, with sunsets and sunrises in between as cushions.

Have you ever been in charge of the sunrise since you have been in this world? How many times did you dress up the night in the garment of the day? How many times did you make the streaks of light on the cheeks of the ocean grow into the bright sun? Oh, you may have had some courses in Astronomy, or studied some lessons about how the earth revolves and rotates, but just try to really explain how the sun can disappear, fading into the darkness of night, while the reflected light of the full moon lights up the dark night sky.

Since you ponder the problems of life; since you question God about the death of someone near and dear to you; since you are confused because you have had some reverses in your personal life which you cannot understand; since you dropped a stitch in the garment of your attempt to live a perfect life; and instead, you made some human mistakes. Tell me, God is asking, what would happen if I dropped a stitch in keeping the planet earth in place? What if I hiccupped while moving the sun through the sky, or suppose I made a misstep in keeping the planets in orbit around the sun, or what if I took a nap and let the constellations and galaxies get off their proper paths? Tell me Job, where were you when I set up these systems? You want to take over and be God, tell me where were you when I laid the very foundation of the universe? Where were you when the morning stars sang together and all the sons of God shouted for joy? Where, where were you?

II.   What Do You Know About Rain, About Water?

1.   Oh, that's an easy one isn't it? We all have seen rain. We understand the need for rain. There are some who can predict the rain, but Job, since you know so much tell me about the rain. Does the rain have a father? What mother gave birth to the snow? Out of whose womb did the ice come forth? What great gardener gets up early every morning and waters the fields all over the world with dewdrops? Or, Job, where do the dewdrops come from anyway?

We call water H-2-O. We store it in reservoirs and purify it. We say that it is odorless, colorless and tasteless. Yet, with all our knowledge, we can't make it as pure as God keeps it in the earth.

My first trip to the country was as a boy of eight. While being led through the woods we came upon something which I had never seen before. It was called a brook and the person told me to lie down over it, take water in my hand and suck it up. And do you know what it was like? It was the best water I had ever tasted. Water from a brook, direct from the earth; pure, good.

Today, a booming business is where big companies bottle water straight from the ground, put it in bottles and sell it to us because it is good. Somehow, with all of our so-called

wisdom, we still pollute much of what we touch. But, God
makes it pure and rich and good, straight from the ground. So,
with all of our twenty-first century smarts, how much do we
really know about water?

2.   Speak up Job, talk to me. You question me about little
things which break your heart. Well, your pain matters to me,
but I will ask you some big questions. I won't hold it against you
if you can't answer, but what gives you the right to challenge
my authority? Can you control the clouds and make it rain? Do
you have any power over the place of water in nature? Can you
stop the rain, like I did in Elijah's time when it didn't rain for
three years? Can you make it rain forty days and nights, like I
did in Noah's time?

You know so much about life, tell me, tell me, if you can, about
the rain, the snow, the dew drops. You think you know so much.
You can't understand simple things, yet you question me about
the wonders of nature. What do you know about evaporation,
purification and condensation? Tell me if you can, how the sun
can shine down on a dirty mud puddle and through the process
of evaporation, draw it up into the heavens. Tell me if you
can, how that dirty water can be purified through the clouds,
begin to fall as rain, but in mid-air, it is frozen into snowflakes,
and falls clean, pure and white on the mountaintop. It is as
different as night and day, having gone from mud puddle to
snowflake, through the purification systems of Almighty God.
Do you know how it is done? Tell me, were you there in the
beginning when I made it happen?

Yes, I wonder if any of us understands that the same procedure
can take place in the lives of suffering, sinful human beings.
We can be as filthy as the mud puddle. But grace can shine
on us, and draw us up into the arms of Jesus. When you see
us again we don't look the same. We can be as different from

what we used to be, as the mud puddle is different from the snowflake.

Hymn writer Robert Lowry said it this way:

What can wash away my sin? Nothing but the blood of Jesus
What can make me whole again? Nothing but the blood of
Jesus.

Oh! Precious is the flow, That makes me white as snow
No other fount I know, Nothing but the blood of Jesus.

For my pardon this I see, Nothing but the blood of Jesus
For my cleansing, this my plea, Nothing but the blood of Jesus.

Conclusion

When I ask, "How do you fathom the questions of God?" possibly I am asking the wrong question. The one answer is an obvious no. God is so high, so wide, so deep, so incomprehensible that we surely know that God's questions are beyond our ability to even attempt to answer.

But, we need to remember that it is God who asked the questions. So, perhaps God likes to ask us human beings questions which we cannot possibly answer. Perhaps God wants us to admit that we don't have the answers. Do you remember that time when Israel was in the midst of that great and terrible exile in Babylon? Things seemed to be so awful that it seemed that a whole nation was in trouble. Things were terrible. Her people were being amalgamated. Her altars had been destroyed. Her idea of God and the way to worship God had been desecrated. And what did God do but take his excitable prophet, the one given to dramatic expressions and in a vision set him down in the midst of a valley of dead dry bones. Oh, I know you remember Ezekiel, looking at those rider-less horses, those wheel-less chariots, those bones scattered all over the valley. And what does God do but ask him a question which he could not hope to answer. That question was, "Son of Man, can these bones live?"

And Ezekiel looked around and began to stammer. Lord, you are asking me if these bones can live. Lord, if I say yes, I am in trouble because I don't know how it can happen. And Lord, if I say no, I am in trouble because I do know that there is nothing that You can't do. So, Lord, in answer to your question I must simply say, this. Oh Lord God, you know!

And then, you know what happened. I know you did not forget. You heard it as a child in Sunday School. You have heard preachers preach about it ever since you have been in church.

God ordered Ezekiel to speak to those dry, dead, disintegrating, rotting bones in the valley and they began to move around. Then they got together. You have heard the song about it: the head bone's connected to the neck bone, shoulder bone, back bone, hip bone, leg bone, knee bone, shin bone, ankle bone, foot bone. Saying, hear the word of the Lord. And then God spoke and life came into the bones and they lived. A vision, yes. A picture of what could happen to Israel, yes. But more than that: It is a picture of what God can do and what God will do in the challenging seasons of our lives.

Somebody knows what I am talking about. Somebody has been in a strait-jacket. Somebody, possibly you, are in a dry bones season of your life right now. And the message I have for you is that God will ask you questions. But, that's not all. For God will come to you in your darkest hour. God will step in just when you need him most. The words of this old Gospel song, author unknown, depict it best:

When my trials seem more than I can bear
When I seem burdened down by the weight of care
Jesus steps in, just when I need him most.

When I've gone to my extreme
And all I've done is in vain it seems,
Jesus steps right in, just when I need him most.

Has God done just that for you in the past? Did God step in, even if you didn't understand how the sun rose or why the moon changes and how the tides rise? God will still come when you are in trouble. If you don't, realize that it's God's timetable or method. But when you look back you now understand that it was God making a way for you. An old gospel song said it this way:

You can't hurry God,
You just have to wait
You have to trust Him and give him time
No matter how long it takes.
He's a God that you can't hurry
He'll be there don't worry
He may not come when you want him
But I declare, He's right on time.

Job was sick so long
Until the flesh fell from his bones
His wife, cattle and children
Everything he had was gone
He said you put these afflictions upon me
Why don't you come on and see about me

You can't hurry God,
You just have to wait
You have to trust Him and give him time
No matter how long it takes.

He's a God that you can't hurry
He'll be there don't worry
He may not come when you want him
But I declare, He's right on time.

WHEN YOU ARE IN A STRAIT-JACKET
Sermon 14: "How Do You Fathom Questions of God?" Pt 2 of 3
By Rev. Dr. James D. Peters, Jr.

"Would you indeed annul my judgment? Would you condemn Me that you may be justified? Have you an arm like God? Or can you thunder with a voice like His? Look on everyone who is proud, and bring him low; Tread down the wicked in their place." (Job 40: 8, 9 & 12 NKJV)

As we move toward the conclusion of the spiritual drama of the book of Job, I have divided the questions raised by God to Job, into three categories. This is the second. These questions which form our text today point clearly to your need, our need, to fathom questions from God about the difficult subject of good and evil. So, God begins another round of questions to Job. Job is still reeling from the queries about nature, things which he could not hope to fathom. Job confesses that he is out of his league. He, in fact, admits his weakness and his inability to engage in verbal combat with God. He says, behold I am vile, how can I answer you? I will place my hand over my mouth and ask no more questions. I spoke once, but I will not answer, twice, but I will proceed no further.

Between the first and the second parts of the divine discourse, at the end of which Job seems to humble himself, we find a short statement from the Almighty. Here is a brief reply on Job's part, which, however, is insufficient. God calls on Job to make good on his charges. (verses 1-2). Job declines, acknowledges himself to be no match for God, and promises silence and submission for the future. But, God determines that something more is needed to bring Job to where he needs to be, so the questioning continues.

Job has been overcome by questions from God about the powers of nature. He thus has become aware of the folly of his previous judgments of God and realizes that his presumption has been wrong.

Job is given every opportunity of taking advantage of his plea for a chance to argue with God. God said, "Gird up your loins now like a man." (Job 40:7 KJV) God then inquires of Job if he has any questions that he really wants to ask. God is ready, yes even anxious to hear him.

Job seems humble, but it is not yet a sense of true humility that fills the spirit of Job. Human beings may never know their own real limitations until they really come close to understanding the greatness of God.

Now, the supreme Jehovah stoops to become His own spokesperson for the singular purpose that He might set things straight in the mind of Job, and all of us. By asking questions, God could dispel the incorrect image Job had tried to create about the equity or inequity of God.

Job's statement, "once, have I spoken, but I will not answer, yea twice, but I will proceed no further" (Job 40:5 KJV), was his way of confessing that in the past, he had talked too much. He is still not saying that what he said, or asked was wrong. God now goes into the second round of questions. In light of all that you now know about Job and his feelings about God,

I ask you, "How do you fathom questions from God? I have two points.

I. Are You Ready To Take My Place?

1.   Verse 6 gives us these words, "Then answered the Lord unto Job out of the whirlwind, and said, 'Now prepare yourself like a man; I will question you and you shall answer Me'." (Job 40:7 NKJV) Job seems to be saying, Lord, I have spoken out of turn and I will say no more. He is not saying you are right, [at this point] all he is saying is I don't want to talk about it anymore.

Many difficult and confounding questions had been asked of Job by God in Chapters 38 and 39. Now in this chapter, God wants some answers to them and Job only offers silence. God challenges Job to vie with Him on the subject of justice and fairness. God asks "Would you indeed annul my judgments?"

Jehovah is saying by this that Job's conduct, in maintaining that he (Job) had been right, really involved two tremendous assumptions. 1. That he (Job) could govern the human beings more justly than God. 2. That he (Job) was a more righteous being than His maker. Sometimes we human beings might do well to keep our lips closed when dealing with divine things which we do not understand.

Of Job, God is asking, "Will you condemn me so that you may be justified?" (Job 40:8b NASB) Come on Job, since you know so much, tell me, are you ready to take my place? God is talking to us also.

2.   Do you have an arm like God? The might of God's arm is often dealt with in scripture. God brought Israel out of Egypt with a mighty hand and outstretched arm. God is always clothed with majesty and strength. Job is challenged to array

himself the same way if he feels that he is ready to take God's place. God is saying, Come on Job. I set up the bar of justice and determined how human beings would be judged. Job, you think you can do better? Stand up, answer me, take your best shot. I am that I am. Do you still want to take my place? Where is your arm of power? Where is your voice like thunder? Where is your hand of mercy? Where are you, Job, answer me if you think you are ready to take my place.

II. How Will You Handle Good and Evil in the World?

1.   This was a difficult time for Job. With God asking questions, momentarily he seems to forget about his pain. [Talking to God can sometimes make your pain take a back seat.] Job was probably saying within himself, "Lord, how can I answer, how can I fathom the depths of your questions? I still have questions about my suffering, but I know I went too far when I asked for a chance to debate with you. From the questions you raise, I am still perplexed by the mystery of suffering, but Lord, I am no longer in a mood to make any claim against You." Job can no longer maintain that God owes him health and wealth. His religion is undergoing a process of purification as little by little he abandons his aloof, self-righteous attitude. He is still not fully ready to confess that he did wrong, because he had not yet grasped the full importance of his failing confrontation with God. Yet, he is not confessing that his silence is the result of his limited knowledge of divine things.

The author of this book of Job skillfully succeeds in suggesting that humility does not come easily to a person of Job's caliber. A person who has been buffeted by pain and suffering may not always be humble. This second series of questions is indeed justified. Job's full understanding of the questions of God are not yet complete.

2.   On the question of dealing with the proud, God is saying to Job just this. "If my moral government does not satisfy you, improve on it. Put down the wicked ones whom you say that I allow to prosper," for that is what Job said in Job 24:2-23, "crush them into the dust. Do what you accuse me of not doing." God is also saying to Job, you claim that you are a powerful man among men. Now, admit that you cannot rival me in nature so get busy and you set good and evil straight in the world. If you can do that, with your own power and wisdom, with your own right hand you can save yourself. (verse 14)

What God is saying to Job is this. When you have done what I am now challenging you to do, then you may attempt to contend with me. You will have established your own independence from me, and I will acknowledge you as one who is fully able to argue with me. So, come on Job, gird up your loins like a man, show me your power, show me your wisdom in dealing with questions of good and evil, of equity and inequity.

3.   Job, since you seem to feel that you know so much about the constant battle between good and evil in the world, tell me how you would go about handling the proud. You know who I mean. Those stuck up, self-righteous, people who live in a sophisticated society of sanctified snobs. You know who I mean, those people who are so heavenly-minded that they are no earthly good. You know who I mean, those who gag at a gnat and swallow a camel. You know who I mean, those who think that they cannot make mistakes. How would you handle them, Job?

Now, if God was asking Job about dealing with the spiritually proud, what does that say to you and me? Oh yes, we know Job was a good man, even God said so. But is it possible that Job had too much pride? For you see, all have sinned. You see, we tend to focus on big sins, but God is always telling us to watch out for the so-called little foxes which spoil the vines.

Those little sins which get between us and God. Those sins which we can see so well in others, but not in ourselves.

Tell me Job, if you were the judge of heaven and earth, would you allow it to rain on the just and the unjust? If you were a District Court Judge would you be a hard-liner and give everybody the maximum sentence? Or would you give repeat offenders a second and a third chance? What kind of Judge would you be? Some people would like to castrate all rapists, execute all murderers and confine all drug addicts in some faraway facility. That is, until someone in their own family got in trouble.

This is what God is asking Job. This is what God is asking you. In your strait-jacket times you question the fairness of God. You even say that God is unfair. But, how would you handle justice?

A little rhyme says it this way:

> *There is so much bad in the best of us*
> *And so much good in the worst of us*
> *That it hardly becomes any of us*
> *To talk about the rest of us.*

Conclusion

One thing we need to learn about God is that God deals with human beings on the level of grace, even when they deserve only justice. God gives suspended sentences when we deserve time, pardons instead of convictions. God is the author of mercy. So when we hurt and in our pain, try to say that God is unfair, remember that if God had not extended mercy to us, the question is this. Where would we be?

The message that God gave to Job out of the whirlwind, has been given to us through Jesus Christ. Through Christ he let us know that God is love. Even in your strait-jacket times and when you can't fathom the heavy divine questions of God, just remember that God is all powerful.

God speaks to us: through these songs which we sing in church, or used to sing in church, or those songs which we hear sometimes and enjoy even though we never went to church. Through nature and art and music and sermons we are beginning to get a clear picture. That magnificent image of God Himself, is not for condemnation, but for salvation.

Through His questions, God is also telling Job that you don't understand who it is that is talking to you. I am the one who caused to be everything that is. Before there was a when or a where or a then or a there, I was. It was I who stepped out into the darkness of eternal chaos and said, "Let there be light." (Genesis 1:3 KJV) It was I who spat out the seven seas. I batted my eyes and the lightning flashed. I clapped my hands and the thunder rolled. I carpeted the earth with grass and dotted the hills with trees. I flung the stars to the most far corner of the night. I kneeled down in the dust, gathered it up and made man. I am God. No matter what happens, I am God.

The songwriter, Harry Fosdick, in 1930 said it well:

God of grace and God of glory
On Thy people pour Thy power.
Crown Thine ancient church's story
Bring her bud to glorious flower.

Grant us wisdom, Grant us courage
For the facing of this hour,
For the facing of this hour.

Set our feet on lofty places
Gird our lives that they may be
Armored with all Christlike graces
In the right to set men free.

Grant us wisdom, grant us courage,
That we fail not man nor Thee.
That we fail not man nor Thee.

WHEN YOU ARE IN A STRAIT-JACKET
Sermon 15: "How Do You Fathom Questions of God?" Pt 3 of 3
Rev. Dr. James D. Peters, Jr.

"Can you draw out the Leviathan with a hook, Or snare his tongue with a line which you can lower. Can you put a reed through his nose, Or pierce his jaw with a hook?" (Job 41:1-2 NKJV)

You have noticed that the scripture is from the New King James Version of the Bible. In most of the versions, including the King James and the Living Bible, the text selected uses crocodile. A large number of critical bible experts see this passage as referring to a variety of large, dangerous animals. My connecting of this beast mentioned in this chapter 41 as a picture of death is the result of my own research. Included in that research, was the reading of a sermon which I had saved for many years—Dr. Galbraith Hall Todd's sermon which was printed in "Christianity Today" issued November 26, 1956. In this sermon written many years ago, his research agreed with my own that the reference here is to a terrible creature, which for Job in his strait-jacket situation, and for us in our human situation, is death. Dr. Todd's sermon was entitled "Three Questions to a Man in Trouble". The last of these questions was, "What do you know about death?"

To fathom means to get to the bottom of, or to understand thoroughly. We have used this subject for these last three sermons dealing with the many questions which come from God to Job, and which are found in Chapters 38, 39, 40 and 41. These questions from God are indeed classic poetry, but they are much more than that. They represent God, the creator, asking Job the complaining creature, why certain things happen in life. Job has had the audacity to suggest that God did not know how to govern the universe, since he, Job, was suffering and he was a good man. In covering these four chapters I have placed these many questions from God into just three categories. What do you know about Nature? What do you know about good and evil in the world? And, What do you know about Death? Today we look at the last of these three questions. I have two points.

I.   What is this Strange Animal?

1.   The word Leviathan is mentioned in many other places in the bible and is associated with several kinds of beasts or monsters. The best modern critics regard it as a very large crocodile. A Leviathan, the Interpreters Bible tells us, is different from an ordinary crocodile because it is a sea monster which cannot be captured, and is associated with the forces of primeval chaos. Like all human beings, Job is totally helpless in the presence of this creature.

God, in asking Job questions, is ending the argument in high gear. God is asking Job about his superior knowledge, asking if he can do anything with something as frightening as this creature. Who are you Job, to stand before me and claim to know about the great mysteries of life? Tell me what you know and understand about this monster of the sea?

In the mythological imagery of Egypt and the ancient East, the hippopotamus and the crocodile always represented death and the realms of the dead. In the symbolism of the Coptic Church in Egypt in the early centuries, Christ is depicted standing upon a crocodile. So this passage is seen by many, myself included, as a question from God to Job about death.

2.   For we know so little about that soft, fascinating sleep which human beings call death. We know so little about that strange land in the narrow divide between life and death, so little about the here and the hear-after. Yet, how often we, like Job, try to question God about facts of life and death.

Job, in the classic cursing which he did in Chapter 3, curses the night in which he was conceived, and the day he was born. What do you really know about death?

Yes, you know that it is cruel, uncompromising, unpredictable and seemingly final. You know that it changes a living body into a lifeless corpse. It ends the fellowship of many decades. It crushes the dreams that many share for a better, longer life down here. It makes tears flow which sometimes you can't seem to control. It scares you deep down inside, because you know that you, too must go.

But, beyond that, what do you know about death? Only a few in the whole history of the adventure of human beings on this earth have returned from the grave. And they didn't file a report, or do a study or write a thesis.

Everybody is affected, rich, poor, white, black, young, old. Human beings have conquered space, even walking on the moon. We have explored the depths of the ocean and climbed to the top of the highest mountain, even without oxygen. But what do we know about death? How do we fathom questions from God?

3. "Come on Job," God says, "answer me." Will you put a reed in the nose of this creature or pierce his jaw with a hook? Can you make him talk to you? Will he speak soft words to you? Will he make a covenant with you? Will your friends make a banquet for him? Are these idle questions from God? I don't think so. Is God mocking Job? Not really. God is continuing his cross examination of Job after Job's many questions to God.

Again, I ask you to focus that in the ancient world, Leviathan was a symbol of death. To many of us who, in our seasons of distress and grief; in our times when trouble seems to come through a tear-stained eye; to those of us who are subjected to instant problems which can come to us without warning; for us to we who have come to understand that our entire lives can be rearranged through no fault of our own; we who are tempted to cry out to God, "Lord this is not fair." God is asking us, and Job, "How much power do you have over life and death?" Would you treat death like a toy, and play with him like a bird if it were in your power to do so?

II. What Do We Really Know About Death?

1. This passage focuses on a string of questions, aimed at convincing Job of how helpless he is in the presence of such a frightening creature. How could you catch him? And even if you could, what would you do with him? The suggestions are rhetorical. What would you do, make him a servant, a pet, sell him?

The most courageous man would not be so insane as to stir up a beast with his bare hands. How could anyone be so foolish as to stand up against God, as Job has done? We can feel the force of these powerful questions from God. How do we deal with them?

The argument of the superior strength of God, is made not to discourage men from trying to ask God questions, but to focus on God's capability of managing the affairs of the universe. This is a long illustration, covering this entire 41st Chapter. This lengthy question about the most terrifying animal was placed at the end of the questions to provide a terrific climax to the questions from God to Job and to all of us. The dread of the beast is mentioned in verse 10, mentioned again in passing in verse 25, and forcefully driven home in the concluding lines in verses 33 & 34.

2.   The lessons here for us are: A. The impossibility of contending with God. If no man can hope successfully to encounter a huge crocodile, how foolish must it be to think of striving against God. B. The sovereignty of God's procedure in the world. If God, in fashioning so powerful a beast had acted solely on his own will, was it not probable that God might in the same manner, act in connection with us. C. The probability of God's works in providence being marked by wisdom. If, in the structure of an amphibious creature, there was so much protection by virtue of his coat of overlapping scales, would not the design of human beings include some protective gear? Learn the great power of God, who can control the fiercest of creatures, even though we humans may be afraid of them. Most of all we must develop the wisdom of faith, which always trusts where it cannot understand.

3.   Leviathan the Terrible. This terrible monster has a whole chapter to himself. His portrait is painted on a broad canvas, and it is as full of life and movement as it is of form and color. Representing the Leviathan, it is a picture of a most terrible animal. And is not the adventure of our loved ones with death just as terrible sometime? You see, I do know about death. He is terrible. He came and got my mother, my father, my sister and one of my daughters. I know him. I am sure that you do too. If not yet, you surely will. But God can chase away some

of our fear, even when we cannot understand. Even when we are tempted to be the most fearful, God can make adjustments in our circumstances and our spiritual support systems, so we could sing in another generation, and even today, "I am not afraid today. Deep in my heart I do believe, we shall overcome some day."

You see, human beings are all of one species, of one great family, and therefore we are all brothers and sisters regardless of race, creed or color. We have a moral nature, and can discern a higher right than that of might and power. Human beings have, or can have, religion and faith, which teaches them that their own instincts and wills are to be subordinate to the will of God.

God is King of Kings. It would be a fearful thing if the power to destroy which is entrusted to the larger animals had been given to them without limits or restraints. But the powerful animals, like the crocodile are all obedient to the Lord who rules over all the works of animal life. They could not rebel against their God-given instincts even if they wanted to. So, God gives us power, but it has boundaries, it has limitations. For no matter how much we tend to think of ourselves, or how high and lofty our positions may seem, we will be called into account before our Supreme Maker. We too, just like Job is now being called to account in these closing chapters of his story, will also be called. We might ask astounding questions, even challenge the equity of God, but some day, God may well demand from us, answers to God's questions, of us. Therefore, it will be well for us to look up above for all greatness and rule to that one supreme authority which has been revealed to us in Almighty God.

Conclusion

What do we know about Death? I mentioned that few have come back, and they did not talk about it. But, poets, preachers, playwrights and authors, and the writers of hymns and gospels songs have looked at death and their words tell us much. Alfred Lord Tennyson looked at Death, and said:

Sunset and evening Star, and one clear call for me
And may there be no moaning of the bar, When I put out to sea.
Twilight and evening bell, and after that the dark
May there be no moaning of farewell, when I embark.

Henry Wadsworth Longfellow looked at death and said:

Tell me not in mournful numbers, Life is but an empty dream
And the soul is dead that slumbers, And things are not what they seem.
Life is real, life is earnest, and the grave is not its goal.
Dust thou art, to dust returneth ; was not spoken of the soul.

William Cullen Bryant wrote:

So live that when thy summons comes,
To join that innumerable caravan
which moves to that mysterious realm,
where each shall take his chamber in the silent halls of death.
Go not like a quarry slave at night,
Scourged to his dungeon
but sustained and soothed by an unfaltering trust,
approach thy grave as one who wraps the drapery of his
couch about him and lies down to pleasant dreams.

Thomas A. Dorsey said:

I am tired and weary, but I must toil on

Till the Lord comes to call me away
Where the morning is bright and the Lamb is the light
And the night is as fair as the day.

There will be peace in the valley for me someday
There will be peace in the valley for me, I pray
No more sorrow and sadness or trouble will be
There will be peace in the valley for me.

Samuel Stennett put it this way:

When shall I reach that happy place
And be forever blest?
When shall I see my Father's face
And in His bosom rest?

I am bound for the promised land,
I am bound for the promised land
Oh, who will come and go with me,
I am bound for the promised land.

And lastly, Lucie Campbell wrote this:

Not just to kneel with the angels,
Nor to see loved ones who've gone
Not just to drink at the fountain,
Under the great white throne

Not for the crown that He giveth,
That I'm trying to run this race
All that I want up in heaven,
Is just to behold his face.

A driver leaves the house in the morning. He travels in both the dark and the light, in the blistering heat and in the biting cold. He travels on many kinds of roads. Some may have pot holes. On others he may have to deal with detours. But he keeps driving on, no matter the climate, congestion or unexpected conditions. Finally, late in the day, he pulls into the driveway next to the house. A key is turned and the motor no long hums. A button is pushed and the lights no longer shine. But the person driving gets out of the vehicle and goes into the house.

And so I, a driver, did start out in the morning of my life. I have traveled in the darkness of the early day and the bright sunlight of the midday moments. I have had to drive in the heat of the noonday sun and in the chilling cold of the evenings. Difficult roads were filled with some of life's heavy traffic, highway construction and traffic lights which will not work. Yet, I had to drive on, no matter where life led. Finally, at the end of the day, as I turn into the driveway beside the house. A key is turned and the heart no longer beats. A button is pushed and the eyes no longer shine. But the real me, gets out of the vehicle and goes into the house.

For we know that when the house of this earthly tabernacle is dissolved, we have another building from God, a house not made with hands, eternal in the heavens, eternal in the heavens.

"Oh death, where is thy sting? O grave, where is thy victory?" *(I Cor 15:55 KJV)*

WHEN YOU ARE IN A STRAIT-JACKET
Sermon 16: "What Do You Do
When God Delivers You?"
By Rev. Dr. James D. Peters, Jr.

"And the Lord restored Job's losses when he prayed for his friends. Indeed the Lord gave Job twice as much as he had before." (Job 42:10) "I know that You can do everything, And that no purpose of Yours can be withheld from You. You asked, Who is this who hides counsel without knowledge? Therefore I have uttered what I did not understand, Things too wonderful for me, which I did not know. Listen please and let me speak; You said, I will question you, and you shall answer Me. I have heard of You by the hearing of the ear, But now my eye sees You. Therefore I abhor myself, And repent in dust and ashes." (Job 42:2-6 NKJV)

In these verses in Chapter 42, Job backs down. He no longer wants to argue with God. He has no further questions about the meaning of, or reason for, his suffering. He repents for having asked the questions which he posed. His repentance included the acknowledgement of God's power and the admission of his own ignorance. He cried out, "I repent in dust and ashes. I uttered what I understood not, things too wonderful for me." It has been said that the hardest words in the English language, or any language to say are, "I was wrong." Job was saying just that.

Also note here that God has some words for the so-called friends of Job. In verse 7b God says, "My wrath is aroused against you and your two friends, for you have not spoken of Me what was right, as My servant Job has." Think about it. It matters to God how his children are treated and what people say about you. You owe Job an apology for the things you have accused him of doing. God will not forsake you or allow people to beat up on you when you are down and out. And that is what they had done. These men, who tormented Job, had urged him to admit that he was a great sinner and was getting what he deserved. They came to Job now, and Job prayed for God to forgive them, and God heard Job's prayers for them, and God forgave them. This prayer of intercession helped Job's friends. It helped Job and, if we understand the implications found here, it will help all of us too. The Bible tells us that, "The Lord accepted the prayers of Job."

You need to know that Job being out of his strait-jacket, will not necessarily mean that you will come out of yours now. But it does reflect and represent that there is a way out of terrible situations. It has to be done on God's timetable. And while you may want to, as the old song says, "You can't hurry God. I have two points in the development of the text.

I. God Will Bless You Spiritually

1.   Job, now having found peace and forgiveness from God, could not afford to be indifferent to his disappointing and misguided friends. Even though they had hurt him, when they came to him for forgiveness and prayer, he responded. He prayed. God heard, answered and they were blessed.

But more than that. Perhaps, just perhaps, Job's complete forgiveness by God was contingent on his own complete forgiveness of his friends. Follow my thinking on this as you read verse 10. "And the Lord restored Job's losses when he prayed for his friends. God gave Job twice as much as he had before." How did Job get back into fellowship with God? Was it by repenting? Yes. But, more than that, he who needed the forgiveness of God also had to extend forgiveness to those who had done him wrong.

We can only ask for that which we are willing to give ourselves. Love is the only collateral for other acts of love. Love and forgiveness, to be full, must be reciprocal. If you are hard, and cold, and demanding the last full measure from every person with whom you deal, you can expect the same thing back. The basis of God's forgiveness toward you is measured by your ability to forgive others.

Why, you even pray to God, don't you? And you ask for God's love and forgiveness to you to be measured by the extent to which you forgive others. Haven't you used the model prayer given to us by Jesus? I am sure that every Christian has quoted that prayer given to us by Jesus "And forgive us our debts as we forgive our debtors." (Matthew 6:12) Did you know what you, were saying? Be careful about asking God to treat you the same way you treat other people. And, notice the footnote on The Lord's Prayer. This clause in The Lord's Prayer is the only one followed with a clear footnote. "For if you forgive men their trespasses, your Heavenly Father will also forgive you. But if you do not forgive men their trespasses, neither will your heavenly Father forgive your trespasses." (vv. 14-15)

2.   So, how did Job find spiritual restoration? He found it by repenting, and by confession, yes, he did. But it was also by putting love into action—By going beyond the demands of divine love and asking God to forgive those who had treated him wrong. If you want to be restored, if you want to get out of the strait-jacket of bitterness and hatred and resentment toward those who treat you wrong, then you forgive them. You need to have some mercy, and you love until it hurts, and you

WHEN YOU ARE IN A STRAIT-JACKET

give until you give out, and then you give some more. God is saying that if you forgive others, I will forgive you. Do you want to be restored? God is still restoring: materially, yes, but spiritually first.

3.   Job's words, found way back in Chapter one, after the first shocking losses, give us hope. He said, "The Lord giveth and the Lord taketh away, blessed be the name of the Lord". That remains a great statement of faith and is a great response to human tragedy. But, let us not forget that the reverse is also true. The same God who permits the taking away, also restores. You may have been, or you may be, down but you are not out. For the God who takes away, also gives back. There are times when we need to be reminded that there is more than one turn in the road. In spite of all of his suffering, in the closing of this beautiful story, we find that God gives back more than was taken away.

We have spent a long time sharing in the suffering of Job as he wore his strait-jacket. But let us not forget that Job won out in the end. The old song was right, for Job, and for you and me when it said:

I'm so glad, trouble don't last always.

Divine reversal comes through. Job's troubles have come to an end. It was a long journey and the strait-jacket was tight and painful. But, trouble ends someday. There is a terminal at the end of the line of suffering. God will bless you spiritually.

II.   God Will Bless You Materially

1.   We have talked about Job's spiritual restoration. Now, let me say a word about his material restoration. I feel a deep sense of excitement as we look at how God restored and blessed his servant, Job. The overwhelming goodness of God expressed

here leaves Job gasping for breath. The exceeding abundance of God's blessing leaves Job totally astonished.

What this tells us about God is that God does not simply mend and patch up the broken life. God heals and renews and blesses with super abundant kindness. God's blessings are not always both spiritual and material. [It is possible for God to bless you spiritually now and you may have to wait for the material, the financial blessings.] But when God does bless us in both ways, it is truly great and wonderful. God is able to bless all of the ways. There are times when God opens the windows of Heaven, pours out such a blessing, that we do not have room to receive it. What Job received was beyond his wildest dreams. When you are hurting, you only pray for the pain to go away. But when you look back on your grief, after God has blessed, you are often surprised to find that God not only took away the pain, but gave you some extras as well. So, let us look for a few minutes at how God gave to Job, and will give to us, some extras, some God-given extras.

2. What shocking words we find in verse 11. "Then all of his brothers and sisters, and all of those who had been his acquaintances before, came to him and ate food with him in his house; and they consoled and comforted him for all the adversity that the Lord had brought upon him. Each one gave him a piece of silver and each a ring of gold." [Yes, that's verse 11].

What? We are almost horrified to find out on the last page of the book, that Job had sisters and brothers, as well as other friends during the whole time of his affliction. Yet, not once during all of his suffering did they attempt to comfort him. By benign neglect, too often, we often fail to respond to the needs of those around us, even those in our own families. Think about it. When things are going good, friends and relatives are in abundant supply. But when days are dark and circumstances bad, often no one is around. This can make you bitter. But, Job shows no bitterness. His grand spirit does not focus on the loneliness he felt. He ignores the faults of his fellows. Like a true child of God, he accepts their gifts when he does not need them, even though they did not come when a cup of cool water would have been a great blessing.

As Christians we must learn that our generosity is a sign of the health of the soul. How healthy is your soul? If you are only nice to those who are nice to you, what credit do you get? Anyone can do that. But here Job shows us the true measure of a saved soul: Compassion.

The victory and happy end of Job's life are a message to every Christian. God will leave you better off than when He found you. The Lord will make a way somehow. What does that song say? "There's a bright side somewhere."

Job had been put to the test. His faith held out. His patience prevailed. He had won in the end. You may lose some battles, some contests, some games, and some tests. That's life. But in the great game of life, you can be a winner in the end. You don't have to make the playoffs, or be named to, or even make the all-star team. The great sports writer Grantland Rice said:

For when the one Great Scorer comes to mark against your name,
He writes, not that you won or lost, but how you played the game.

Sometimes we get so caught up in obtaining spiritual blessings, that we forget that God has things too. The spiritual blessing comes first. Look at what God did for Job. God gave him double what he had lost. Before he lost everything, Job had:

Rev. Dr. James D. Peters, Jr.

7 thousand sheep . . . . Ended up with 14 thousand
3 thousand camels . . . . . . Ended up with 6 thousand
500 teams of oxen . . . . . . Ended up with 1 thousand
500 female donkeys . . . . . . Ended up with 1 thousand. (Verse 12)

Now God gave Job a new family. Before, Job had seven sons and three daughters. After his recovery, his new family consisted of seven sons and three daughters. Some will notice that the new family is not double, but the same number he had before. God doubled the sheep and camel, the oxen and the donkeys, why not the children? I have a suggestion of the answer to my question.

We need to remember that those who have left us by death, are not really gone forever. They may well be somewhere in the presence of God, which, could mean that fellowships broken by death may be restored. [Of course, I don't know how or when.] But, I do know that all things are possible with God. There are some concepts of Heaven in which Job would then have fourteen sons and six daughters.

Conclusion

God gave Job double what he had lost. And that is what God can do for all of us in His own way. Job had been rich in the beginning of this great drama. In the end, he was filthy rich. God has it all. It all belongs to Him. He can give to those who are His own, that which belongs to Him. And the least we can do while we live, is return to Him some of that which He has given to us. For, we are His people and the sheep of His pasture. (Psalm 100:3b)

Now, what do you do when God delivers you? I don't know what you do, I can only testify about what I plan to do. The words are not mine. I heard them sixty years ago from a lady whose name was Clara Ward, in "How I Got Over" she sang:

Soon as I can see Jesus,
The Man that made me free.
The Man that bled and suffered
And died for you and me.

I thank Him because He taught me.
I thank Him because He brought me.
I thank Him because He kept me.
I thank Him because He never left me.

Thank Him for the Holy Bible.
Thank Him for good old revival.
Thank Him for heavenly vision.
Thank Him for old time religion.

I'm going to thank Him for all He's done for me.

EPILOGUE

A man of God from whom I have learned throughout the years of my ministry, Dr. Gardner C. Taylor said:

"Whenever men and women have thought seriously about the issues of life, they have pondered these words and sentiments of the book of Job, this ancient drama of suffering and of a suffering shot through by a presence, of suffering examined and suffering redeemed." This whole book of Job is an accurate transcript of what human life is all about. It is a biopsy, a sample of living tissue, of what our human condition is all about. It speaks of tears and laughter, of joy and sorrow, of health and sickness, of prosperity and adversity, of sunshine and storms, of fair weather and foul, all touched by the living presence of the everlasting God."* (The words of Gardner C. Taylor's Book 3, pages 64-65)

The book of Job is indeed one of the most unusual, fascinating, dramatic and challenging stories in the Bible. Its author had a depth and wealth of knowledge about God and about human problems and reactions. In several places, he has Job in a position of questioning God, yet, somehow, trusting in God's ultimate reality and equity.

While I have preached and have done Bible studies from Job, this is quite different. I delivered a series of 27 sermons in this series from my pulpit, beginning in August 1994. At that time I was personally passing through a season of a special kind of grief. It was not some immediate problem which could be solved by some short-term remedy. I was passing through a season which would be long-term with many implications and which would touch the lives of many people.

One of my goals for this sermon series is to comfort people who are passing through long-term situations through which there will be no short-term solutions. It's for people who are facing incurable diseases like Parkinson's disease, Lou Gehrig's disease, Multiple Sclerosis, and others. And not only sickness, but it's also for people who are preaching to people in desperate situations—those who do not know where to turn. It may be for people who have recently lost loved ones. It could be for people who feel about to give up. Often people in times like these, question God. Some even give up on God.

Some people need to see an example of someone who has walked where they are walking and lived through what they are going through. I have seen so many people who wander through these emotional strait-jacket seasons as hopeless victims of life's unpredictable circumstances with pessimism. They often see their situations as a "drift into disaster".

I am totally convinced that there are many who can be helped by looking at Job, thinking about the message, the adventure and the journey of Job. I found that to be true when I preached these sermons. I was told over and over again by so many who were themselves passing through trying times, that this series was a great help to them. Even after all these years, I still hear comments about these sermons from the book of Job.

The story is told of a little girl whose mother gave her brushes and water color paints. She immediately began to paint on her canvas. After a while her mother asked what she was painting. She answered, a picture of God. But, her mother explained, no one knows what God looks like. The little girl replied, "They will when I get through".

Well, every time I write or preach a sermon, this is my goal. That when I am finished, people will have a picture of what God looks like.

I had a professor, Dr. Andrew Fowler, who enhanced my already deep appreciation for great poetry. He once remarked that just as people look at a baby laughing and say that the baby is playing with the angels, great poets felt the same way. He then quoted James Russell Lowell with a verse from "The vision of Sir Launfal" which says:

Not only around our infancy
Doth heaven with all its splendors lie;
Daily, with souls that cringe and plot,
We Sinais climb and know it not.

Thank God for the journey and His blessings.

James D. Peters, Jr.